GANDHIAN JOURNALISM
Is It Relevant Today?

GANDHIAN JOURNALISM
Is It Relevant Today?

D.V.R. MURTHY

KANISHKA PUBLISHERS, DISTRIBUTORS
NEW DELHI-110 002

KANISHKA PUBLISHERS, DISTRIBUTORS
4697/5-21 A, Ansari Road, Daryaganj
New Delhi-110 002
Phones : 2327 0497, 2328 8285
Fax : 011-2328 8285
E-mail: kanishka_publishing@yahoo.co.in

First Published 2010

ISBN 978-81-8457-181-3

PRINTED IN INDIA

Published by Madan Sachdeva for Kanishka Publishers, Distributors, 4697/5-21A, Ansari Road, Daryaganj, New Delhi-110 002, Typeset by Sunshine Graphics, Delhi, and Printed at Rajdhani Printers, Delhi.

Acknowledgements

I desired to work on a topic Gandhi and journalism four years back, and I could not succeed in my mission. Though I have been longing to study the relevance of Mahatma Gandhi to the present day, I have not been able to move forward owing to other engagements. However, six months back, my colleague, friend and convener, Gandhian Studies Centre, Andhra University, Dr. A.B.S.V. Ranga Rao insisted me to study Gandhi's relevance to the present day journalism, I have agreed to do so, and the result is the present work, Gandhian Journalism: Is it Relevant Today? The study sponsored by the Gandhian Studies Centre has been helpful for me to complete the work. I am extremely thankful to Dr. Ranga Rao for goading me to take up the present work. Otherwise, the present work would not have seen the light of the day.

I am also thankful to Dr. G. Anita, teacher associate, Department of Journalism and Mass Communication, Andhra University for helping me in the data collection. I also thank Mr. Y.D. Ramdas, journalist and a research scholar for correcting the drafts many times.

I am extremely thankful to my wife, Dr. Padma, MD, physician for her cooperation and encouragement for timely completion of the work.

Visakhapatnam

D.V.R. Murthy

Contents

1
Gandhian Journalism

As for giving ideas, I have originality. But writing is a bi-product; I write to propagate my ideas. Journalism is not my profession.

– Gandhiji in Harijan, August 18, 1946

Gandhian journalism began in India nearly 140 years after the first newspaper was started by a European, James Augustus Hickey in 1780. Since then, very few publications came into existence, which were launched both by the Britishers and Indians. Prominent among them were Rajarammohan Roy's *Sambad-kaumadi* which was launched in 1822 while Fardoonji Murzban started the vernacular newspaper in Gujarati, *Bombay Samachar* in the same year. It was interesting to note that all the English dailies had 4000 subscribers, out which 125 were Indian subscribers in 1823 (Murthy, 2004: 37).

Mahatma Gandhi was instrumental in launching, *Indian Opinion*, in 1903 a weekly which started publication in four languages–English, Hindi, Tamil and Gujarati with an intention to serve all Indians in South Africa. Two close associates of Gandhiji, Madanjit Vyavaharik and Manshuklal Hiralal Nazar launched *Indian Opinion* on June 4, 1903 while the latter a journalist from Bombay was looking after the editorial function of the weekly. The intention of the journal was to act as a voice of the Indian community and to improve their lot, and thus the journal did not have any commercial leanings. As the two gentlemen could not run the journal, the responsibility fell on the shoulders of Gandhiji, who took over the journal in October 1904. His friend, Albert West who gave up his business as a printer was managing it, while Gandhiji was editing the journal with the sole intention of educating and mobilizing Indians through the weekly columns on various aspects of life. Gandhiji's mission was to portray the sufferings of every Indian in South Africa and indicated the line of duty that every Indian must follow in order to win his elementary rights (Bhattacharya, 2002: 44). The journal, in particular carried the popular biographical sketches of eminent men in many parts of the world such as Count Tolstoy, Abraham Lincoln, George Washington and Iswar Chandra Vidyasagar. Also he supported the publication financially. In his autobiography, he noted that lack of funding to the weekly forced them to discontinue the publication in Tamil and Hindi. He outlined the three objectives of the journal, *Indian Opinion* (Bhattacharya, 2002: 44-45). They were: (1) to make Indian grievances known to the Governments in South Africa and Britain and to the people of India, (2) to make the Indians in South Africa aware of their own shortcomings and try to overcome them, and (3) to eliminate the prevailing distinctions between Hindus and Muslims and among Gujaratis and Tamils and others. Therefore, Gandhiji said, "I poured out my soul in its columns and expounded the principles and practice of *satyagraha* as I understood it." The journal had a circulation of 3500 and every Indian was eagerly waiting to receive it every week (Nanda, 1998: 98).

Gandhiji, in fact, wrote only two books, '*My experiments with truth*' in Gujarati and '*Hind Swaraj or Home Rule*' which was written in Gujarati was translated by him into English. In the preface to the book *Hind Swaraj*, he said:

> It (*Hind Swaraj*) was written in 1908 during my return voyage from London to South Africa in answer to the Indian school of violence and its prototype in South Africa. I came in contact with every known Indian anarchist in London. Their bravery impressed me, but

> I felt that their zeal was misguided. I felt that violence was no remedy for India's ills, and that her civilization required the use of a different and higher weapon for self protection. The Satyagraha of South Africa was still an infant hardly two years old. But it had developed sufficiently to permit me to write of it with some degree of confidence. What I wrote was so much appreciated that it was published as a booklet... In my opinion it is a book which can be put into the hands of a child. It teaches the gospel of love in place of that of hate. It places violence with self sacrifice. It pits soul force against brute force. It has gone through several editions and I commend it to those who would care to read it.

Hind swaraj used the technique of dialogue between the reader and the editor. The purpose of adopting of such dialogue seemed to be that Mahatma did intend to clarify the doubts that would linger in the mind of the reader. He answered many queries posed by the reader such as education, civilization, culture and so on. Answering a query of the reader in *Hind Swaraj*, Gandhiji explained the objectives of newspaper. He said 'one of the objectives of the newspaper was to understand popular feeling and to give expression to it; another was to arouse among the people certain desirable sentiments, and the third was fearlessly to expose popular defects.' While explaining the objectives of the newspapers, he further, commented on the power of the press.

> "In the very first month of *Indian Opinion*, I realized that the sole aim of journalism should be service. The newspaper press is a great power, but just as an unchained torrent of water submerges whole countryside's and devastates crops, even so an uncontrolled pen serves but to destroy. If the control is from without, it proves more poisonous than want of control. It can be profitable only when exercised from within. If this line of reasoning is correct, how many of the journals in the world would stand the

test? But who would stop those that are useless? And who should be the judge? The useful and the useless must, like good and evil generally, go on together, and man must make his choice.

As soon as he returned from South Africa in 1915, Gandhiji started his political life. However, he launched three newspapers during 1919-20 defying the Indian Press Act.[1] Although the Act barred new publications, he boldly launched *Satyagrahi* (in Hindi and Gujarati), *Nava Jivan* (Gujarati), and *Young India* (English).

Consequent upon the World War I and the massacre at Jullianwalla bagh, B.G. Horniman, the English editor of the *Bombay Chronicle*, was vehemently condemning the British administration for the atrocities and supported the National Movement. As a result, Horniman was deported to Britain. The directors of the *Bombay Chronicle* who were running the other journal, *Young India* requested Gandhiji to take over the journal. Gandhiji agreed on the condition that the editorial office would be shifted to Ahmedabad from Bombay as he set up an ashram at Ahmedabad which would require his guidance. As he purchased a printing press, Navajivan Publishing House to publish his monthly, *Navjivan*, he would bring out *Young India* from Ahmedabad. He gave a note to the subscribers in the first issue of *Young India* on October 8, 1919:

> ... The editing of "*Nava Jivan*" has been a perfect revelation to me. Whilst "*Young India*" has a little more than 1200 subscribers, "*Nava Jivan*" has 12000. The number would leap to 20000 if we would but get printers to print that number. It shows that a vernacular newspaper is a felt want. I am proud to think that I have numerous readers among farmers and workers. They make India. Their poverty is India's curse and crime. Their prosperity alone can make India a country fit to live in. They represent nearly 80 per cent of India's population. The English journals touch but the fringe of the ocean of India's population. Whilst therefore I hold it to be the duty of every English

knowing Indian to translate the best of the English thought in the vernacular for the benefit of the masses, I recognize that for a few years to come i.e. until we have accepted Hindustani as the common medium among the cultured classes and until Hindustani becomes compulsory in our schools as a second language, educated India, especially in the Madras Presidency must be addressed in English.

But I will not be party to editing a newspaper that does not pay its way. "*Young India*" cannot pay its way unless it has at least 2500 paying subscribers. I must appeal to my Tamil friends to see to it that the requisite number of subscribers is found, if they wish to see "*Young India*" continued. The more so now, because the proprietors of "*Young India*" have decided to give up all advertisements. I know that they have not been entirely if at all converted to my view that a newspaper ought to be conducted without advertisement. But they are willing to let me make the experiment. I invite those who wish to see "*Young India*" free from the curse of advertisements to help me to make the venture a success. The Gujarati "*Nava Jivan*" has already demonstrated the possibility of conducting a newspaper without advertisement soiling its pages. What a financial gain it would be to the country, if there was for each province only one advertisement medium-not a newspaper—containing innocent unvarnished notices of things useful for the public. But for our criminal indifference, we would decline to pay the huge indirect taxation by way of mischievous advertisements. Some readers who are interested in the purity of journalism recently sent me a most indecent advertisement extracted from a well-known newspaper. I have refused to soil the pages of "*Nava Jivan*" by reproducing it. But anyone turning to the advertisement sheets of even leading journals can verify the aptness of my criticism.

He did not accept advertisements and believed that the newspapers should survive on the revenue from subscribers. The circulation of *Young India* went up to 45000, and his articles were effective (Ramakrishna, 2002: 21). However, *Young India* was closed in 1932 owing to repressive acts of the British administration.

The thought of having another weekly was lingering in Gandhiji's mind when he was in prison in Poona on account of Civil Disobedience Movement (Bhattacharya, 2002: 94). Though he was in prison, he established Harijan Sevak Sangh and asked the Sangh to publish *Harijan*. On February 11, 1933 *Harijan* was published as a weekly, at the request of Gandhiji which carried, 'Gandhiji's views on untouchability, village sanitation, rural reconstruction through village industries, women's education, women's rehabilitation, basic education, and the upliftment of all (*sarvodaya*) through employment for every able bodied person (Vilanilam; 2005: 81). For instance, Gandhiji wrote in *Harijan* on February 27, 1937: "I believe in the proper education of woman. But I do believe that woman will not make her contribution to the world by mimicking or running a race with man. She can run the race, but she will not rise to the great heights she is capable of by mimicking man. She has to be complement to the man."

With such educative contents, the print order of the weekly was 10000. However, in response to the censorship imposed on the newspapers, Gandhiji suspended the publication of *Harijan* in November 1940 with an article, "good-bye", and within a gap of one year, he resumed the publication in January 1942. In eight months of its' resumption of publication, Gandhiji went to prison on August 8, 1942, and immediately the administration closed down the weekly. But it came back to life after a lapse of three and half years on February 10, 1946 (Bhattacharya, 2002: 200). As Gandhiji was upright in his attitude, he wrote in *Harijan* in July 1947: Perhaps we may have to close the *Harijan*. My mind rebels against many things that our leaders are doing. Yet I do not feel like actively opposing them. But how can I avoid it if I am running a paper? Further, he wrote: Sardar, I feel that *Harijan* should now be closed. It does not seem to me to be right to give contrary guidance to the country (Bhattacharya, 2002: 201).

Though Gandhiji viewed that the duty of the newspapers was only to serve the people, he used *Young India* to resist the Britishers boldly in not compromising with any aspect related to the freedom of India, and also the freedom of the press. In the face of mounting hostility against the British administration, the government brought in the Press Act of 1910 which imposed heavy security deposit to open a printing press, and thereby muzzle the freedom of the press. However, Gandhiji stood firmly for the freedom of the press, and two cases reported below illustrate how Mahatma argued his cases related to contempt of court, and sedition which he accepted eventually to go to jail.

Contempt of Court

As a journalist, Gandhiji never shirked from the responsibility of carrying the burden of proof, and he favoured objectivity in the news reports and also exhorted the newspapers to abide by objectivity instead of favouring other methods to escape the law. He boldly published a letter against the judge to express the truth. He stood by his conviction in questioning the judge's attitude. He was prepared to face the consequences of violating the rule, and in the face of tough stance of the judge, he firmly argued his case to resist contempt of court. In the two issues of *Young India*, he published articles which attracted the law of contempt. On March 10, 1920, in *Young India*, contempt of case proceedings were reported with a heading, **'Was it contempt of court? Proceedings against Mr. Gandhiji and Mr. Mahadeo H. Desai'**. Two judges Marten, and Hayward Kajiji were hearing the contempt case against Editor Gandhiji and Publisher Desai of *Young India* for publication of a letter addressed by Kennedy, District Judge of Ahmedabad to the Registrar of the High Court complaining of the conduct of certain Satyagrahi lawyers of Ahmedabad. In April 1919, Judge Kennedy found that certain lawyers in Ahmedabad had signed the Satyagraha pledge, and he asked them to explain why their Sanads should not be cancelled for their having signed the pledge. He did not consider their explanation satisfactory and hence addressed a letter to the Registrar of the High Court on April 22, 1919. In consequence, two notices were issued by the High Court to the lawyers concerned. A copy of Mr. Kennedy's letter was given by the Registrar to Divetia, pleader for one of the lawyers, who handed the same to Mr. Kalidas J. Jhaveri, one of the Satyagrahi lawyers, who in turn handed it Mr. Gandhiji. On August 6, 1919 the letter was published in *Young India* with a heading "O'Dwyerism in Ahmedabad" along with an article commenting on the letter with a heading "Shaking Civil Resisters." As soon as the proceedings were completed, the Registrar addressed a letter to Mr. Gandhiji directing him to appear before the Chief Justice's Chamber to give an explanation as regards the publication of the letter. Mr. Gandhiji replied by telegram explaining his inability to attend on the appointed date as he was going to the Punjab. The Registrar replied saying that the Chief Justice did not wish to interfere with Mr. Gandhiji's appointment and that a written explanation would do. Gandhiji was asked to publish an apology in the paper, which was refused by Gandhiji. Following his refusal, the judge declared the publication of the letter would come under the contempt of court. On the judgment of the High Court, Gandhiji stood firmly on the ground saying he would honour the independence of the journalist and would go to any extent to undergo punishment. The article appeared on March 24, 1920 in *Young India* with a heading, **contempt of court** as follows:

> The long-expected hearing of the case against the editor and the publisher of Young India in connection with the publication of a letter of the District Judge of Ahmedabad regarding Satyagrahi Lawyers and my comments thereon has been heard and judgment has been pronounced. **Both the editor and the publisher have been severely reprimanded.** But the court did not see its way to pass any sentence upon either of us. If I dwell upon the judgment it is only because I am anxious as a Satyagrahi to draw a moral from it. I wish

to assure those friends who out of pure friendliness advised us to tender the required apology, that I refused to accept their advice not out of obstinacy but because there was a great principle at stake. **I had to conserve a journalist's independence and yet respect the law.** My own reading of the law was that there was no contempt committed by me. But my defence rested more upon the fact that I could not offer an apology if I was not prepared not to repeat the offence on similar occasion. Because I hold that an apology tendered to a court to be true has to be as sincere as a private apology. At the same time I owed a duty to the court. It was no light thing for me to refuse to accept the advice of the Chief Justice especially when Chief Justice was so very considerate in the correspondence with me. I was on the horns of a dilemma. I therefore decided not to offer any defence but simply to make a statement frankly and fully defining my position, leaving it to the court to pass any sentence it thought fit in the event of an adverse decision. **In order to show that I meant no disrespect of the court and that I did not desire to advertise the case I took extraordinary precautions to prevent publicity** and I venture to think that I succeeded eminently in convincing the court that behind my disobedience-if it was disobedience, there was no defiance but perfect resignation, there was no anger or ill-will but perfect restraint and respect: that if I did not apologize, I did not because an insincere apology would have been contrary to my conscience. I hold that it was about as perfect an instance of civil disobedience as it ever has been my privilege to offer. And I feel that the court reciprocated in a most handsome manner and recognized the spirit of civility that lay behind my so called disobedience. The luminous judgment of Justice Marten lays down the law, and decides against me. But I feel thankful that it does not question the propriety of my action. Justice Hayward's judgment recognizes it as an instance of passive. i.e. civil resistance and practically makes it the reason for not awarding any sentence. Here then we have an almost complete vindication of civil disobedience. Disobedience to be civil must be sincere, respectful, restrained, and never defiant, must be based upon some well understood principle, must not be capricious and above all must have no ill will or hatred behind it. I submit that the disobedience offered by Mr. Desai and myself contained all these ingredients.

Sedition Case

Gandhiji published three articles in Young India dated September 29, 1921 with a heading 'Tampering with Loyalty', another article on December 15, 1921 with a heading 'the puzzle and solution', and the third article on February 23, 1923 with a heading 'Shaking the Manes.' In these articles, he severely criticized the British administration, and asked the people to rebel against the government, and in particular the Indian sepoy to rebel against the government. For instance, December 15, 1921 contained the following passage.

"A Puzzle and Its Solution"

Lord Reading is puzzled and perplexed. Speaking in reply to the addresses from the British Indian Association and the Bengal National Chamber of Commerce at Calcutta, His Excellency said, "I confess that when I contemplate the activities of a section of the community, I find myself still, notwithstanding persistent study ever since I have been in India, puzzled and perplexed. I ask myself what purpose is served by flagrant breaches of the law for the purpose of challenging the government and in order to compel arrest." The answer was partly given by Pandit Motilal Nehru when he said on being arrested that he was being taken to the house of freedom. We ask arrest because the so called freedom is slavery. We are challenging the might of this government because we consider it activity to be wholly evil. We want to

> overthrow the government. We want to compel its submission to the peoples will. We desire to show that the government exits to serve the people, not the people the government. Free life under the government has become intolerable, for the price exacted for the retention of freedom is unconsciously great. Whether we are one or many, we must refuse to purchase freedom at the cost of our self-respect or our cherished convictions. I have known even little children become unbending when an attempt has been made to cross their declared purpose, be it ever so flimsy in the estimation of their parents. Lord Reading must clearly understand the non-cooperators are at war with the government...

Because of these writings, a case of sedition was registered against the editor, M.K. Gandhiji and the publisher, Shankarlal Ghelabai Banker on March 18, 1922 in the District and Sessions Court, Ahmedabad. The charges were "bringing or attempting to excite disaffection towards his Majesty's Government established by law in British India, and thereby committing offences punishable under Section 124A[2] of the Indian Penal Code." When the charges were read out in the court, the judge, C.N. Broomfield called upon the accused to plead to the charges. He asked Gandhiji whether he pleaded guilty or claimed to be tried. Gandhiji pleaded guilty to the charges and Banker too pleaded guilty to the charges. The judge wished to give his verdict immediately, but the advocate-general, J.T. Strangaman insisted that the due process of law must be followed. The advocate-general requested the judge to take into account "the occurrences in Bombay, Malabar and Chauri Chauri, leading to rioting and murder." In respect of Banker, the advocate-general said that the second accused, the offence was lesser as he published them, and did not write them. Therefore, the advocate-general asked for a substantial fine in addition to imprisonment as might be possible. However, the judge asked Gandhiji that "would he like to make a statement." Gandhiji agreed to give a statement, and the judge asked for a written statement to be recorded.

Gandhiji made an oral statement, which was followed by a written statement (see written statement in Appendix). Gandhiji said:

> Before I read this statement I would like to state that I entirely endorse the learned advocate-general's remarks in connection with my humble self. I think that he was entirely fair to me in all the statements that he has made, because it is very true and I have no desire whatsoever to conceal from this court the fact that to preach disaffection towards existing system of Government has become almost a passion with me, and the advocate-general is entirely right when he says that my preaching of disaffection did not commence with my connection with *Young India* but it commenced much earlier, and in the statement that I am about to read, it will be my painful duty to admit before this court that it commenced much earlier than the period stated by advocate-general... it is impossible for me to disassociate myself from the diabolical crimes of Chauri Chaura or the mad outrages of Bombay...I do not ask for mercy. I do not plead any extenuating act. I am here, therefore, to invite and cheerfully submit to the highest penalty that can be inflicted upon me for what in law is a deliberate crime, and what appears to me to be the highest duty of the citizen. The only course open to you, the judge, is, as I am going to say in my statement, either to resign your post, or inflict on me the severest penalty if you believe that the system and law you are assisting to administer are good for the people...

Further Louis Fischer (1994: 259-260) recorded as follows:

> When Gandhiji sat down, Mr. Justice Broomfield bowed to the prisoner, and pronounced sentence 'The determination of a just sentence,' the judge declared, "is perhaps as difficult a proposition as a judge in this country could have to face. The law is no respecter of persons. Nevertheless, it will be impossible to ignore

the fact that you are in a different category from any person I have ever heard or am likely to have to try. I would be impossible to ignore the fact that in the eyes of millions of your country men, you are a great patriot and a great leader. Even those who differ from you in politics look upon you as a man of high ideals and of noble and even saintly life."

The judge then announced that Gandhiji must undergo imprisonment for six years, and added that if the government later saw fit to reduce the term 'no one would be better pleased than I'. Mr. Banker received one year jail and fine of one thousand rupees.

On hearing the sentence, the Mahatma rose and said that the sentence 'is as mild as any judge could inflict on me, and so far as the entire proceedings are concerned, I must say that I could not have expected greater courtesy.'

The two cases reported above illustrate that Mahatma Gandhiji never compromised on the principles he enunciated throughout his life. As said earlier, Gandhiji considered journalism as a by-product of his activities, and newspaper was a vehicle for him to propagate his views. He firmly asserted that he was writing these articles only to awaken the Indians and to rouse desirable sentiments in them against the British rule while engaging more number of people with nationalism.

NOTES

1. 'With the repeal of vernacular Act in 1881, printers and publishers had to register their newspapers with local officials, and publications had to carry their names and addresses. Press Act in 1910 (repealed in 1922) and 1931 attempted to keep newspapers under some form of legal control, but by 1931...it was understood that it was politically impossible to leave decisions about newspapers simply to officials, the court had to be given a role' (Jeffrey, 2003: 186).
2. Section 124A of Indian Penal Code. Whoever by words, either spoken or written, or by signs, or by visible representation,

or otherwise, brings or attempts to bring into hatred or contempt, or excites or attempts to excite disaffection towards, the government established by law in India, shall be punished with imprisonment for life, to which fine may be added, or with imprisonment which may extend to three years, to which fine may be added, or with fine.

Explanation 1: The explanation "disaffection" includes disloyalty and all feelings of enmity.

Explanation 2: Comments expressing disapprobation of the measures of the Government with a view to obtain their alteration by lawful means, without exciting or attempting to excite hatred, contempt or disaffection, do not constitute an offence under this section.

Explanation 3: Comments expressing disapprobation of the administrative or other action of the Government without exciting or attempting to excite hatred, contempt or disaffection, do not constitute an offence under this section.

2

Gandhiji, Journalism and Values

The editor of a daily newspaper when he begins writing his leader does not weigh his words in golden scales. He may be betrayed into a hasty word. Must he pay for it even though he did it obviously in good faith without malice and in the public interest?

—Gandhiji, Young India, August 7, 1924

Gandhian journalism emerged from the values and philosophy practiced and propagated by Mahatma Gandhiji in his life and through his publications viz., *Indian Opinion, Harijan* and *Young India.* With courage of conviction, Gandhiji applied the principles in his life and also in journalism and could bravely write his quest for truth or experiments with truth in the modern era narrating his experiences while boldly facing the poignant situations to achieve his goals. Essentially, he believed that newspapers should have values when they were launched with a view to serving the people.

Gandhiji and News Values

In the determination of news, journalists use different criteria keeping in view the target audience. Prominently news values are used as a yardstick to determine the nature of newspaper. Broadly, newspapers are classified as broad sheets and tabloids, and broad sheets are considered to be elite, serious and thought-provoking in terms of contents, while tabloids focus on non-serous and flimsy issues. For instance, tabloids focus on sex, scandal and surprises to attract the reader's attention. Moreover, the news values are the bedrock of the profession on which the credibility and character of a newspaper rely upon to establish a relationship with the readers. In a study done by Masterton (1998) of news values in 69 countries, he found six major news values were universally accepted:

- Consequence (importance, strength of effect),
- Proximity (geographic and cultural),
- Conflict,
- Human interest (stories about ordinary people),
- Novelty (unusual or bizarre events), and
- Prominence (events involving prominent people).

Although he found these six news values as universally accepted, they are interdependent. For example, a conflict in association with prominence occupies prominent place in newspapers. Thus, conflict-prominence or conflict-novelty and so on secures more space in the newspaper columns. However, in another study done by Harcup and O'Neill (2001) suggest that ten news values obtain importance in the present day newspapers. They are:

- Reference to the power elite (individuals, organizations and nations)
- Reference to celebrity
- Entertainment (sex, human interest, drama)
- Surprise
- Good news (rescues, personal triumph)
- Bad news (e.g. tragedy, accident)
- Magnitude
- Relevance (cultural proximity, political importance)

- Follow up stories
- The newspapers agenda.

Thus, it is understood that the news values are kept on changing with the addition of new values to the list of old values. In fact the purpose of a newspaper is to inform the readers the events that take place in a society. Because a newspaper is not like a product to be sold on the basis of price, readers judge the quality of a newspaper in relation to its news content. Since a newspaper never makes an attempt to lose the base of readership, the readers' needs are fulfilled by the supply of news while being accountable to the public. The theoretical view is that social responsibility is an ethical issue for a newspaper. In relation to its role as a public educator, newspapers have certain news values in reporting or selecting an event before it is transmitted to the public. In India, the press is dominated by certain news values in the post-Independent India. Of course, every press system in the world can adopt different set of news values keeping in view the country's priorities or the newspaper's readership profile. Hence, Murthy (2002) summarised the news contents in the Indian newspapers as follows:

1. The Indian Press is influenced by the Western news values of sensationalism, sex, scandal, gossip and conflict. The news values of the third world like development, education, national integration, and social responsibility are relegated to the backseat.
2. Scoop is the most sensational word in the journalistic profession. Journalists vie with each other to out beat their professional rivals rather than to consider their relevance to society.
3. Event reporting is given much importance than process reporting.
4. Newspapers dedicate space to flimsy and non-relevant issues.

Contrary to these news values, Gandhian journalism emphasises on four different criteria of news namely, **culture,**

probity in public life, peace, and development. Gandhiji did not explicitly speak of these news values, however, he laid emphasis on them because of his personal experience derived from his philosophy of non-violence (*ahimsa*), self-reliance (*swadeshi*), self rule (*swaraj*) and truth force (*satya graha*) (Vilanilam, 2005: 80).

Culture

'Geert Hofstede defined culture as that which distinguishes one group of people from another group of life. This broad definition focuses on how the values of a group people are manifested essentially in that group's rituals and symbols. At the centre of culture is a set of societal norms based on values shared by a population that has experienced a common history. These norms in turn foster the development of societal institutions including family, education, government and media' (Mccenzie, 2007: 39). Although many definitions are given to describe culture, Sitaram (1970, cited in Rich and Ogawa, 1998) defined culture as a sum total of the learned behaviours of a group of people, which are generally considered to be the tradition of that people and are transmitted from generation to generation. Further culture involves knowledge, belief, art, morals, law, custom, and any other capabilities and habits acquired by a man as a member of a society (Tylor, 1977). Viewed from this perspective, culture epitomizes the norms of a society, and the people in that society make efforts to preserve it to hand over to the posterity. Gandhiji favoured preservation of Indian culture and had shown the world the 'Indianness' in his physical countenance and through his personal conduct. Gandhiji explained the reason for adoption of loin cloth in *Young India* (April 30, 1931).

> The adoption of the loin cloth was for me a sheer necessity. But insofar as the loin cloth also spells simplicity let it represent Indian civilization. It is a mingling of the cultures represented by the different faiths and influenced by the geographic and other environment in which the cultures have met. Thus

Islamic culture is not the same in Arabia, Turkey, Egypt and India but it is itself influenced by the conditions of the respective countries. Indian culture is therefore Indian. It is neither Hindu, Islamic nor any other wholly. It is a fusion of all and essentially eastern. I had in mind that culture. And every one who calls himself or herself an Indian is bound to treasure that culture, be its trustee and resist any attack upon it.

European civilization is no doubt suited for the Europeans but it will mean ruin for India, if we endeavour to copy it. This is not to say that we may not adopt and assimilate whatever may be good and capable of assimilation by us as it doesn't also mean that even the Europeans will not have to part with whatever evil might have crept into it. The incessant search for material comforts and their multiplication is such an evil, and I make bold to say that the Europeans themselves will have to remodel their outlook, if they are not to perish under the weight of the comforts to which they are becoming salves. It may be that my reading is wrong, but I know that for India to run after the Golden Fleece is to court certain death. Let us engrave on our hearts the motto of a Western Philosopher 'Plain living and high thinking'. Today it is certain that the millions cannot have high living and we the few who profess to do the thinking for the masses run the risk, in a vain search after high living, of missing high thinking.

In *Hind Swaraj*, he elaborated the meaning of culture, and its' effect on human behaviour. Modern civilization, according to Mahatma Gandhiji, makes people materialistic and forces them to concentrate their thoughts upon their bodies and upon the means of multiplying bodily comforts as against culture (Selected Works of Mahatma Gandhi, Vol. VI, 1994: 277). For instance, Gandhiji writing about civilization in *Hind Swaraj*, described it as good conduct. Thus, he explained his concept of life through spinning wheel. In *Young India* on September 17, 1925, he wrote: "The message of the spinning wheel is wider than its circumference. Its message is one of simplicity, service to mankind, living so as not to hurt others, creating an indissoluble bond between the rich and the poor, capital and labour, the prince and peasant."

Probity in Public Life

Gandhiji outlined the basic purpose of newspapers was public service. In serving the people, the newspapers were expected to transmit news that would transform the individual from wrong doing to righteous behaviours. Almost Gandhiji's writings had aimed at moral transformation of the individual while reinforcing moral conduct in him. Writing in *Hind Swaraj*, he opined that 'the tendency of the Indian civilization is to elevate the moral being, and that of the Western civilization is to propagate immorality'. With this view, Gandhiji equated civilization with good conduct in his answer to the reader in *Hind Swaraj*. Through his writings in *Young India* and *Harijan*, he emphasized on prayer as one of the means to purge himself/her from the wrong doing and advised all readers to chant Ram. For instance, he advocated nature cure to keep up sound health in an article through his journal *Harijan* on May 25, 1946. He wrote:

> Nature cure consists of two parts. Firstly, to cure diseases by taking the name of the god or Ramayana, and secondly, to prevent illness by the inculcation of right and hygienic living. The report from the village says that the inhabitants are cooperating with them in keeping the village, clean- I hold that where the rules of personal, domestic and public, sanitation are strictly observed and due care is taken in the matter of diet- and exercise, there should be no occasion for illness or disease. Nature cure implies an ideal mode of life and that, in its turn presupposes ideal living conditions in towns and villages.

Stephen Hay (2005: 149) observed: 'His way of transmuting or perfecting his own conduct, and ultimately finding god, was through tightly interweaving the three strands of soul purifying prayer, self rule and selfless service of others. In 1927 he explained, "I am endeavouring to see God through service of humanity, for I know that God is neither in heaven, nor down below, but in everyone...". On number of occasions, Gandhiji wrote on moral conduct of the individual and 'he believed a spiritually integrated person is no longer a slave of the passions, but is able to go about him or her daily affairs in the light of true self knowledge' (Parel, 2000: 16).

In the present day context, dishonesty coupled with corruption is the root-cause of myriad problems, and the politician and the bureaucrat equally share the responsibility. Kothari (1993) noted with concern that 'a significant portion of citizens did not get enough to eat; did not have a secure roof over their heads or enough clothes to cover bodies. Men, women, and children toil from morning to night ...India's poverty is, therefore, not a poverty of resources. It is a ***poverty of Justice***'. Viewed from Kothari's perspective, poverty of justice was the root-cause of many problems. Stories in the Indian Press abound on dishonesty of politicians and bureaucrats. For instance, Sainath's stories (1996) on poverty adequately reflect the dishonesty of politicians and bureaucrats in siphoning off the money meant for development.

> In August 1995, Prime Minister P.V. Narasimha Rao inaugurated an anti-drought project in Orissa. This one will involve spending Rs. 4,557 crores in six years (over Rs. 750 crores a year) on just a few districts including Kalahandi, Bolangir, and Koraput. Every paisa of that huge sum would be worth spending if it actually fought scarcity and built better infrastructure...In theory, drought-prone blocks come under a central scheme known as Drought-Prone Areas Programme (DPAP). But bringing blocks into DPAP is now a purely political decision. The central allocation for DPAP, a phalanx of other schemes then get money coming in under the Employment Assurance Scheme (EAS), anti-desertification projects, drinking water missions and a host of other schemes. Well, *some* people do benefit (pp. 317-318).

The malady in society is corruption which is rampant everywhere, and although newspapers in India focus on the issues related to corruption, the adequacy of stories need to be more when compared with the other news values such as conflict, prominence and so on. For instance, judiciary too is no exception to this prevailing situation.

Peace

One of the present day news values, conflict obtains a prominent place in day-to-day journalism. Be it a conflict between individuals, communities, states or nations, the news related to such conflicts is treated well, and the newspapers advertently exacerbate the conflict by giving it a different angle in the story. Language used in such reports is acerbic and stimulates further fissures in the groups involved in the conflict. Since objectivity in the news reports is slowly declining, the media reports are apparently seemed to be biased. However, all conflicts are not per se bad or uncalled for, and some conflicts certainly yield good results. Thus, media's role in conflicts is to bridge the gap between parties involved and strive for resolution. Thus, the key concept in peace journalism is truth and reconciliation, mediation or negotiation paving way for peace (McGoldrick, and Lynch, 2000). In relation to promotion of peace, Gandhiji emphasised on conflict reduction, and worked towards that end. Gandhiji advocated peace though the publications and advised and admonished both parties involved in conflict to find an amicable solution. Writing about non-violence in Young India on August 11, 1920, he professed the philosophy in an article, 'The doctrine of the sword'

> ...I am not a visionary. I claim to be a practical idealist. The religion of non-violence is not meant merely for the *rishis* and saints. It is meant for common people. Non-violence is the law of our species as violence is the law of the brute...**Non-violence in its dynamic condition means conscious suffering. It does not mean meek submission to the will of the evil-doer, but it means the putting of one's whole soul against**

> **the will of the tyrant.** Working under this law of our being, it is possible for a single individual to defy the whole might of an unjust empire to save his honour, his religion, his soul and lay the foundation for that empire's fall or its regeneration...And I am not pleading for India to practice non-violence because it is weak. I want her to practise non-violence being conscious of her strength and power. No training in arms is required for realisation of her strength...**My service is dedicated to service of India through the religion of non-violence which I believe to be the root of Hinduism.**

Development

In the Gandhian journalism, development or rural development was given importance in view of the fact that Gandhiji was keen on rural development which would play a key role in national development. Further, Gandhiji continually emphasized the necessity for identification with the villagers, who represented the masses of India that their attitudes might be understood and their needs be met. If Gandhiji is understood in right perspective; his comments in relation to development seem highly relevant.

> We must identify ourselves with the villagers who toil under the hot sun beating on their bent backs and see how we would like to drink water from the pool in which the villagers bathe, wash their clothes and pots and in which their cattle drink and roll. Then and not till then shall we truly represent the masses and they will, as surely as I am writing this, respond to every call... "Because I recognize no God except the God that is to be found in the hearts of the dumb millions... and I worship the God that is Truth or Truth which is God through the service of these millions." (Cited in Dalton, 1999: 59)

Although the Indian Press is not complacent about reporting about development, the frequency of reporting is not encouraging (Murthy, 2000). India is in a process of development and the progress of the nation depends on the society as a whole. Yet, majority of the population suffer from acute poverty. For instance, Dhar, (2009) observed that 'globally, diarrhoea causes 5000 child deaths everyday with the number in India standing at 1,000. As far as the non- health implications are concerned; 443 million school days are lost each year due to poor hygiene and sanitation. It also affects girl's enrolment in school. Only four of the 10 girls enrol complete eight years of schooling in India because of lack of separate toilets and water which is a necessity, particularly after they attain puberty. Lack of facilities also reinforces insecurity among women–risking their health, pride and dignity besides harassment. In India, 35 per cent of rural schools do not have toilets and 20 per cent do not have drinking water facilities. Over 6.6 million people still defecate in the open as only 54 per cent of the rural population has toilet facilities'

Gandhian Journalism and Ethics

Ethics in the profession are only guidelines, which are necessary in the process of information dissemination. These ethics relate to language use, and the means adopted in securing information for ensuring objectivity and fairness in presenting facts to the public. Collection and dissemination of information is the duty of the press. Because, the press as a mass communication channel operates in a public sphere for the benefit of the readers, the actions of the press are expected to be above ground. The public scrutinizes the actions of the press on all occasions and expects the press to reflect values and ethics of the profession. In the process of collection and dissemination of information, the press adopts different means to obtain information and occasionally suppresses news from the public because of extraneous reasons. The press is, therefore, expected to have certain norms and ethics in the collection and dissemination. Former Press Council of India Chairman P.B. Sawant (2001) noted that the code of ethics all over the world emphasizes the following: *(a)* honesty and fairness, *(b)* reply to critical opinions, *(c)* objectivity in reporting, *(d)* prohibition to receive gifts, *(e)* respect for privacy, *(f)* distinction between fact and opinion, *(g)* not to inflame hatred, *(h)* not to use dishonest means to obtain information, and *(i)* general standards of decency and taste.

Nevertheless, Sonnenberg (2004) reported a study done in 31 countries on the ethical code, and it was found that journalists adhered to 57 principles and 10 principles were found to be common in all these countries. These 10 principles are: truthfulness, honesty, accuracy of information, correction of errors, prohibition of discrimination on the basis of race/ ethnicity/religion etc., respect for privacy, prohibition to accept bribes or any other benefits, fair means in information collection, prohibition to allow any outsider to have influence on the journalistic work, prohibition of discrimination on the basis of sex/class etc., freedom of speech, expression, comment, criticism, professional secrecy.

Though these codes specifically mention that public accountability and privacy of the individual seem to be important, the media violate them while asking for absolute freedom to discharge its duties. Thus, in many countries, certain elements of free press are regulated such as press freedom, freedom of expression, privacy, libel/defamation/ slander, right to reply, access to public information, discrimination, pre-condemnation and court proceedings, responsibility of the publication, censorship, source protection and minors. Thus, Gandhiji, while favouring press freedom, advised the press to observe self-restraint. He wrote in *Young India* on May 12, 1920:

> Freedom of the press is a precious privilege that no country can forgo. But if there is, as there should be, no check save that of the mild character, an internal check should not be impossible and ought not to be resisted.

Language

Language is a tool of communication for journalists, and use of language in news reports plays a significant role in informing the public about an event. Though a journalist does not witness an event, he or she tries to construct it with the help of information given to him/her by a second party. Sometimes, a journalist may be present at the event; he or she constructs it by understanding it. In such a situation, is the journalist presenting facts to the public? News is a representation of reality that happens in the environment and the language facilitates the projection of reality. In the profession of journalism, use of value-free words is to be practiced to be very objective in reporting an event without any bias. Since the use of language is not mere accidental, they carry the intentions of the writer. Often, the ideology of the writer is understood through his/her writings. Fowler (1991: 5) said 'the contents of newspapers are not facts about the world, but in very general sense ideas'. Thus, the analyses of media discourses can assess the ideological practice of journalists and their representation through language.

Hence, Gandhiji advised the newspapers to give importance to the language being used in the newspapers. The following passage is illustrative of his mind.

> The last, though not the least, question is: What is the duty of a newspaper in a country where there are laws like the "Seditious Writing Act" and the "Defence of Indian Act" to restrict its freedom? In order to get over this limitation our newspapers have evolved a style of writing which makes it possible to interpret what they say on a particular matter, which may seem to fall within the purviews of these Acts, in two different ways. Some have perfected this art to a science. But, in my opinion, this causes harm to our country. People develop a tendency to equivocate and fail to cultivate the courage to speak the truth. It changes the form of the language which, instead of being an instrument for expressing one's thoughts, becomes a mask for concealing them. I am convinced that this is not the way to educate our people. Both people and individuals must cultivate the habit of speaking their minds. Newspapers are in a position to

impart such training to them. The right course, and the one which will ultimately be found to be of the greatest advantage to us, would be that those who are afraid of the above laws and who do not want to get entangled in them should stop publishing newspapers, or that they should frankly state their true views and bear the consequences. Justice Steven has said some where that there can be no hatred in the language of a man who has no hatred in his heart. And if there is any hatred one should frankly express it. In case one hasn't the courage to act thus, one should stop publishing a newspaper. In this lies the good of our people and our country. (From Selected Works of Mahatma Gandhiji, Vol. VI, 1994 : 312).

Objectivity and Truth Telling

Objectivity is defined as an impartial coverage of an event by taking into consideration different shades of opinion. Klaidman and Beauchamp (1987: 61) indicate that 'bias in journalism is a distorted and unfair judgment or disposition caused by the values of a reporter, editor, or institution. Bias is not necessarily ideological, partisan, or manifest over an extended period, and it need not be introduced intentionally'. In order to be objective, a news report must contain the six elements as suggested by Boyer (1981). They are:

- Balance and even-handedness in presenting different sides of an issue;
- Accuracy and realism of reporting;
- Presentation of all main relevant points;
- Separation of facts from opinion, but treating opinion as relevant;
- Minimizing the influence of the writer's own attitude, opinion or involvement;
- Avoiding slant, rancor or devious purpose.

Although objectivity was expected to contain these elements, modern journalists, according to Nelkin (1987), 'no longer believe that real objectivity is possible, but they are expected to approach the ideal of neutrality and unbiased reporting by balancing diverse points of view by presenting all sides fairly, and by maintaining a clear distinction between news reporting and editorial opinion'. Thus, Press Council of India Chairman, G.N. Ray (2007) observed: "one of the controversial issues in modern reporting is bias, in particular on political issues but on cultural and other issues as well."

In order to be objective, newspapers adopt various practices to prevent manipulation of information by giving by-lines, credit line to the sources while writing explicit interpretive stories. Ryan (2001) commented that 'objective journalists are accountable to their audiences, to the highest ethical and professional standards of objective journalism, and, finally, to their employers. They never assume that employers, not themselves, bear the ultimate responsibility for their behaviour'. In spite of these view points, Bagdikian (1987: 179) pointed out that objectivity is losing its sanctity and journalists violate it often. However, bias is classified into two: Structural and partisan (Fico and Freedman, 2008). According to these authors, structural bias is journalistic news values, work routines, organizational resources, and news organization dependencies on other institutions. Partisan bias is journalist's political orientations subverting news organization impartiality in conflict coverage. Thus, nearly hundred years back, Gandhiji noticed that lack of balance or loss of objectivity would be a feature in the new journalism and advised the journalists then to practice objectivity in the face of difficulties. He said:

> Newspapers are meant primarily to educate people, and apprise them of current trends in the history of the world. This is responsible work. Yet we see that readers cannot always depend on the information supplied by newspapers. Often, facts are found to be quite the opposite of what has been reported. If newspaper editors and staff realized that it was their duty to educate the people, they would wait to check

> the veracity of news they print. It is true that, often, they have to work under difficult conditions, and sift the mass of information they receive and then infer hurriedly, within the limited time at their disposal, the true facts in each case. And, yet, I feel that it is better not to publish a particular piece of news until its truth has been definitely established. (From Selected Works of Mahatma Gandhiji, Vol. VI, 1994: 310)

Public Service vs. Profits

Journalism has become an industry in the modern days, and commercialization of the press has been increasingly found in every aspect. Kuldip Nayar (1994) aptly commented that 'the press became more and more commercialized. The old concept of a newspaper representing ideas and nation's ethos had worn out and the profession became an industry'. The contents are aimed at attracting the public and thereby to increase the circulation of the paper. In the process of increasing the circulation, newspapers solicit advertisements from the potential businessmen. Gandhiji's view was that newspapers were meant for public service, they should not compromise on their role in society, and the concept of profits should be relegated to the background. When newspapers solicit advertisements from the businessmen, the newspapers tend to be influenced and they yield to the pressure of those advertisers. Often, adverse news against advertisers is suppressed in support of the advertisers. Being in the service of the people, the newspapers cannot "soil" their pages with such advertisements. For instance, Gandhiji appealed to the readers of *Young India* to support the weekly with their subscriptions, in order to avoid advertisements. Thus Gandhiji observed succinctly:

> 'It is now and established practice with newspapers to derive their main income from advertisements rather that from subscribers. The result is deplorable. The very newspaper which in its editorial columns strongly denounces the drink evil publishes advertisements in praise of drink. We read about the

ill effects of tobacco a well as where to buy good tobacco or which brand of cigarette to smoke in the same newspapers. Or, it may on the one hand, publish a severe denunciation of a certain play and, on the other, elsewhere in its columns, a long advertisement of it. The largest source of revenue is derived from medical advertisement, which is the cause of much harm to our people. They, almost wholly, nullify the other services rendered by newspapers. I have seen the harm caused by the advertisements, for many people are lured into buying the medicines - supposed to increase virility, overcome debility etc. Many of these medicines are those which encourage immortality. It is strange that such advertisements find a place even in religious papers. This custom has been adopted from the West. Whatever the effort, we must either put an end to this undesirable practice or, at least, reform it. It is the duty of every newspaper to exercise care in accepting advertisements for publications in its pages'. (From Selected Works of Mahatma Gandhiji, Vol. VI, 1994: 311-312)

Further, on another occasion, he expressed his displeasure at the modern newspapers. He pointed out: 'It is generally seen that newspapers publish any matter they have without regard to its need or importance just to fill in vacant space. This practice is almost universal. It is so in the West also. The reason is that most newspapers have an eye on profits. There is no doubt that newspapers have done great service to the people and these defects are therefore overlooked. But to my mind, they have done equally great harm. There are newspapers in the West which are so full of trash that it would be a sin to read them. Many create and promote ill-will among people with their prejudices. At times they produce bitterness and strife even between different families and communities. Thus, newspapers cannot escape criticism merely because they also serve the interests of the people. On the whole, it would seem that the gain and loss from newspapers are almost equal.' (Selected Works of Mahatma Gandhi, VI, 1994: 311).

Facts vs. Comment

Interpretative journalism is increasingly becoming a feature of the modern day newspapers. Newspapers because of their inherent weakness of slow disseminators of information as compared to television indulge in interpreting news with their comment. Earlier views which were confined to editorial page at present interpolate with news, and newspapers pass value judgments on the events. One of the ethics in journalism often underlines non-involvement in the events, and the journalist is an objective spectator of the events. Specifically, the emergence of television has posed a problem to viewers in the context of live coverage of issues. The journalist in order to analyze the situation is identifying himself with the situation as in the case of embedded journalism where journalists' trips are sponsored by the source. Objectivity is losing its' relevance as said earlier. Long back Gandhiji observed:

> The reporting of speeches in Indian newspapers is generally defective. There are very few who can write down a speech verbatim while it is being delivered or afterwards from memory. This results in much distortion and interpolation. The best rule would be to send the proof of the reported speech to the speaker for correction and publish its own report of the speech only if the speaker doesn't revise the proof sent to him. From Selected Works of Mahatma Gandhiji, Vol. VI, 1994: 310).

Although Gandhiji was insisting that the information should be cross-checked by journalist before publication, it is not practiced by modern day journalists. One alibi for journalists is that they are rushing to cover many news events, and find less time to verify the facts. In a survey conducted by Murthy (2005), it was found that all the respondents reported that they would not cross-check information in the press notes. Added to it, more than 50 per cent of the respondents informed that they would face a problem with language to express the situation that they had witnessed. Thus Jacquette (2007: 246) explained the reasons for the prevailing environment in the media: 1. news reporters have a complexly interested set of perceptual, personal, and cultural perspectives from which standpoint they collect information, 2. which they must then try to communicate to a readership or audience in a particular choice of texts and images, 3. for persons whose background and presuppositions they may likely have some grasp of, but which will also include persons of very diverse perceptual, personal, and cultural perspectives.

Since journalists emerge from diverse backgrounds, the news reports filed by them reflect the personal variables in them, and thus objectivity suffers most of the times.

3

Gandhiji and Peace Journalism

Non-violence is a power which can be wielded equally by all-children, young men and women or grown-up people-provided they have a living faith in the God of love and have, therefore, equal love for all mankind. When non-violence is accepted as the Law of Life, it must pervade the whole being and not be applied to isolated acts.

—Gandhiji, *Harijan*, September 5, 1936

Gandhian journalism emphasizes on four news values viz., culture, peace, probity in public life, and development. Contrary to these four Gandhian news values, the present day journalism gives importance to four other news values. Culture as a news value has been replaced by consumerism, and the modern newspapers accord high priority to consumer products or its associates. For instance, advertisements contain information related to products such as cosmetics, refrigerators, fans, cookery and so on. An analysis of advertisements in *Young India* revealed that they contained information of textiles and indigenous products. Since Gandhiji was against promotion of advertisement of foreign companies, some of his journals focused on the indigenous companies which promote Indian products. Apart from the advertisements, the news items in the present day journalism deal with market-driven products and the company-sponsored news.

Further, peace as a new value has been replaced by conflict. Conflict news occupies prime place in Indian newspapers, and newspapers too perpetrate conflict between individuals, groups, political parties and governments. A conflict between two State Governments is given utmost importance. For instance, the river water dispute between Tamil Nadu and Karnataka, Andhra Pradesh and Maharashtra and so on fits in the news frames of the newspapers. It is seen in many instances that the newspapers exacerbated conflicts between two communities during the last 30 years in India. One such instance was that the newspaper coverage of Indira Gandhi assassination and the consequent killings of Sikhs in which the newspapers intentionally played up stories to inflate passions against the particular community (Varadarajan, 1999). In fact Gandhiji throughout his life endeavoured to reduce tension between Hindus and Muslims, and he appealed to the two conflicting parties to work for amicable solution. The two journals *Harijan* and *Young India* contained many articles on religion, peace and truth. For instance, he wrote in *Harijan* (January 30, 1937) that "for me the different religions are beautiful flowers from the same garden, or they are branches of the same majestic tree. Therefore they are equally true, though being received and interpreted through human instruments equally imperfect." Such kind of statements inculcated the spirit of oneness in understanding the religious messages among the masses. One can observe in the modern day newspapers that they don't contain such religious discourses or space given to religions is also negligible.

The other news values, probity in public life and development have been replaced by crime and political news respectively. Instead of news related to probity in public life, newspapers prioritize crime news of murders, suicide, thefts and so on. Crime news occupies second place next to politics (Murthy, 2001). Gory description of killings and terrorism related attacks in the public are highlighted in the news pages. Thus, in the process, the readers often express displeasure over such news items. The news is expected to inform the public about an event, but that information is generating negative feelings. Also, it may provoke the members of the public to enact such kind of incidents in real life. In general, crime stories are expected to deter the public from indulging in such criminal activities. The purpose of journalism is to cause altruism in the public, instead of harming the public. Therefore, good journalism is defined as dynamic and gives thorough coverage of important subjects like education, transportation, housing, government's services, and public safety (Murthy, 2004: 2). Exposure of incompetence and indifference of government official while tackling corruption in government can change policies, besides saving government money. For instance, disclosure of information related to hazards involved in environment, health, food and consumer products will save lives. Reporting of cases of the poor, homeless, imprisoned, abused, and mentally retarded can give voice to the voiceless. Conversely, bad journalism is misinformation, which fails to report important news, or reporting depthless, inaccurate and unfair news leaving people dangerously uninformed.

Added to these, development as a news value has a lot of significance in the context of developing countries. India too is in the process of development, and thus development requires more space. Conversely, development is replaced by political news which obtains more coverage and development is relegated to background. A senior journalist and freelance writer Tavleen Singh (1994) comments, "There are other things seriously wrong with Indian journalism like, for instance, our obsession with politics and politicking to the exclusion of real issues. We will, for instance, give you reams and reams on Kanshi Ram's problems with Mulayam Singh Yadav but tell you nothing about the state of governance in Uttar Pradesh."

Peace Journalism

In the context of the debate on news values, peace as a component of news must require a serious attention by the press as practiced by Mahatma Gandhi. Gandhiji practiced peace journalism even before the term was coined by Johan Galtung. Norwegian scholar Johan Galtung first proposed peace journalism in 1970s as a self-conscious, working concept of journalists covering war and conflicts (McGoldrick and Lynch, 2000). Peace journalism identifies itself socially responsible journalism and interprets the events to resolve the conflicts. Thus, peace journalism is defined as a programme or a frame of journalistic news coverage which contributes to the process of making and keeping peace respectively to the peaceful settlement of conflicts (Hanitzch, 2004). Thus, according to Galtung (1998), two modes of reporting such as peace or conflict journalism and war or violence journalism are found in the present day newspapers.

Peace or conflict journalism aims at exploring the background of a conflict with an intention to ascertain the reasons for the conflict. In the process, peace journalism focuses on the solutions to the conflict by giving an equal representation to the views of all the conflicting parties as well as other points of view. The philosophy of peace journalism is to prevent violence and war. Thereby, peace journalism exposes lies, cover-up attempts and culprits on all sides. It also deals with peace initiatives and reports on the post-conflict situation arising out of amicable solution. In contrast, war or violence journalism reports on the conflicting parties while examining the background of the conflict or war. However, this journalism is keen on reporting on the winning chances of one party in the conflict. News coverage begins only when the outbreak of the conflict or war by focusing on the visible consequences of the conflict such as number of deaths, casualties and material damage. Normally, objectivity is lacking in this journalism as the news reports are slanted in favour of one party. It also ensures continuation of the conflict, and therefore the peace initiatives are relegated to the background. This war or violence journalism always awaits the recurrence of violence and sometimes volatile situation of McGoldrick and Lynch (2000) the temporary truce to explode for the media to cover it. Further, offered 17 practices on covering a conflict which includes reporting on the long-term effects of the conflict, orienting news on all sides of ordinary people, and using precise language (See Table 1). For example, one of the 17 practices was to avoid focusing exclusively on the suffering, fears and grievances of one party. This divides the parties into villains and victims and suggests that coercing or pursuing the villains represents a solution. Instead treat as equally newsworthy the suffering, fears and grievance of all sides (McGoldrick and Lynch, 2001). In essence, peace journalism is oriented towards peace, truth, people and solution. When viewed peace journalism from Gandhian approach, Gandhiji advocated peace inter alia non-violence and emphasized on truth force *(satyagraha)* while dealing with people to find a solution to any conflict or a problem. On many occasions Gandhiji used non-violent methods to resolve a crisis. 'In 1922, Gandhiji proposed the establishment of Shanti Sena or peace brigade made up of trained volunteers who would intervene non-violently to prevent communal bloodshed throughout India. This Shanti Sena was later set up after his death and spread from India to other parts of Asia, where they continue to this day, although focused more on rural development than on civilian peacekeeping as such' (Wallis and Samayoa, 2007). Gandhiji advised the practice non-violence with confidence and in an article in *Harijan* (July 6, 1940), he said: "I have been practicing with scientific precision non-violence and its possibilities for an unbroken period of over 50 years. I have applied it in every walk of life, domestic, institutional, economic and political. I know of no single case in which it has failed. Where it has seemed sometimes to have failed, I have ascribed it to my imperfections. I claim no perfection for myself. But I do claim to be a passionate seeker after Truth, which is but another name for God. In the course of that search, the discovery of non-violence came to me. Its spread is my life mission. I have no interest in living except for the prosecution of that mission."

Table–1
Indicators of War Journalism and Peace Journalism

Type of Journalism	*Approach*	*Language*
War Journalism	■ Reactive ■ Visible effects of war	■ Uses victimizing language

Contd....

Type of Journalism	*Approach*	*Language*
	■ Elite-oriented ■ Differences oriented ■ Focuses on here and now ■ Dichotomizes the good and bad ■ Two-party orientation ■ Partisan ■ Zero-sum orientation ■ Stops reporting and leaves after the war	■ Uses demonizing language ■ Uses emotive language
Peace Journalism	■ Proactive ■ Invisible effects of war ■ People-oriented ■ Agreement-oriented ■ Causes and consequences of war ■ Avoids labeling of good and bad ■ Multiparty orientation ■ Non-partisan ■ Win-win orientation ■ Stays on to report aftermath of war	■ Avoids victimizing language ■ Avoids demonizing language ■ Avoids emotive language

Source: Lee, Seow Ting and Maslog, Crispin C, (2005). War or peace journalism? Asian newspaper coverage of conflicts, *Journal of Communication,* June, 311-329.

In order to resolve Hindu-Muslim conflicts, he advised both parties to understand the situation, and the language of Gandhiji reveals the innate power within him. For instance, Gandhiji dedicated the entire issue of *Young India* dated May 24, 1924 to write a lengthy article on "Hindu Muslim Tension, its Causes and Cure." He pointed out that 'two constant causes of friction' with the Muslims were cow slaughter and music. He wrote:

> 'Though I regard cow protection as the central fact of Hinduism (Gandhiji declared), I have never been able to understand the antipathy towards the Mussulmans

> on that score. We say nothing about the slaughter (of cows) that daily takes palace on behalf of Englishmen. Our anger becomes red hot when a Mussulman slaughters a cow. All the riots that have taken place in the name of the cow have been an insane waste of effort. They have not saved a single cow, but on contrary stiffened that backs of the Mussulmans and resulted in more slaughter. I am satisfied that during 1921 more cows were saved through the voluntary and generous effort of the Mussulman than through the Hindu effort during all the previous twenty years, say, Cow protection should commence with us. In no part of the world are cattle worse treated that in India... The half starved condition of the majority of our cattle is a disgrace to us. The cows find their necks under the butcher's knife because Hindus sell them. The only effective and honourable way is to befriend the Mussulmans and leave it to their honour to save the cow. Cow protection societies must turn their attention to the feeding of cattle, prevention of cruelty, preservation of the fast disappearing pasture land improving the breed of cattle...Then there was the music played in Hindu religious processions as they passed mosques at prayer time. Some how, the processions contrived to arrive in front of mosques just when the followers of the prophets were supplicating Allah.

Further, Gandhiji continued that "Hindus sometimes did this with the deliberate intentions of irritating Mussulman. This was as wrong as the Moslem resort to violence in angry retaliation." In the article, he used sober language to express his feeling while advising the two parties to resist from the temptation of resorting to violence and see reason in the situation. Thus, Dalton (1999: 162) commented aptly: "Gandhi's method of *satyagraha* and his inclusive mode of leadership abundantly manifest in his ingenious use of traditional Indian language, images, and symbols which go further than any other single factor to explain the source and dynamics of his power.

His entire style of expression had been cultivated since his early South African experience. It is most evident in his use of words like *satyagraha, swaraj, sarvodaya, ahimsa,* and *harijan*. These were terms which Gandhiji either coined or reinterpreted. Language, though, represents only one element of his style; other components, often less obvious, contributed equally to the way in which he communicated with the Indian people. In his last phase, his style had, after a lifetime of public contact, become largely instinctive; and for this reason, his power over the Indian people reached its zenith."

Furthermore, peace journalism seeks involvement of people to reduce tensions between warring factions. In the Gandhian approach, Gandhiji understood the involvement of the people would be useful to solve communal riots. Thus, he suggested a formation of a peace brigade to reduce frequent conflicts by prescribing a code of conduct to the members of the peace brigade. In *Harijan* (June 18, 1936), he wrote, "sometime ago I suggested the formation of a peace brigade whose members would risk their lives in dealing with riots, especially communal. The idea was that this brigade should substitute the police and even the military. This reads ambitious. The achievement may prove impossible. Yet, if the congress is to succeed in its non-violent struggle, it must develop the power to deal peacefully with such situations." One of the nine-point codes was that the members of the peace brigade "must have a living faith in non-violence. This is impossible without living faith in God. A non-violent man can do nothing save by the power and grace of God. Without it, he won't have the courage to die without anger, without fear, and without retaliation...the knowledge of the omnipresence of god also means respect for the lives of even those who may be called opponents or *goondas.*" Moreover, he appealed to the people that suffering is inevitable to solve some of the problems. He felt that "things of fundamental importance to the people are not secured by reason alone, but have to be purchased with their suffering. Suffering is the law of human beings; war is the law of jungle. But suffering is infinitely more powerful that the law of the jungle for converting the opponent and opening his ears, which are otherwise shut, to the voice of reason" (*Young India*, November 5, 1931). Further, he explained that *goondaism* had to be tackled non-violently by adopting the silent approach, and Gandhiji had an immense faith in the power god, he suggested:

> "The growing *goondaism* of which Bombay had a bitter experience must furnish all with food for reflection. It cannot, it must not be answered with counter *goondaism* than which nothing is easier. What can be easier than to swear harder than one's opponent or to give two blows against one or to organize ten men against five? But this can serve no earthly purpose. And if it can serve any celestial purpose, that abode must be worse than the fabled hell.
>
> Is there then no remedy for the growing evil? The time honoured and well tried method is that of prayer and fasting. But both have to come from the heart. A parrot like repetition of the choicest sentiment and mere starvation of the body would be worse than useless. Prayer an fasting avail where there is a definite consciousness of the presence of God in us, even as we have of friends living under the same roof. Self-deception will not do" (*Young India*, August 13, 1931).

Perhaps the Gandhian approach of peace building seems to be relevant in the recent years. 'In the 1990s, media and peace building have been integrated into the foreign aid and intervention policies of a number of major donors including the members of the European Community, the United States, the United Nations Educational Scientific and Cultural Organization (UNESCO), the World Bank, and many other international foundations'(Howard, 2006). For this purpose, conventional journalism is used to resolve conflicts and traditional channels of communication such as street theatre, posters, radio dramas, and edu-entertainment programmes are also employed to reduce tensions. In the process of peace building too, media can induce peace into the minds of people by constantly reinforcing the idea of non-violence. Gandhiji himself explained it with confidence. He firmly asserted in *Harijan* on November 11, 1938, "Non-violence is like radium in its action. An infinitesimal quantity of it embedded in a malignant growth, acts continuously, silently, and ceaselessly till it has transformed the whole mass of the diseased tissue into a healthy one. Similarly, even a little of true non-violence acts in a silent, subtle, unseen way and leavens the whole society." Thus, Gandhian journalism reflects all the components of peace journalism such as peace, truth, people-centered, and solution to the problem. Gandhiji reiterated that the purpose of newspaper was social service and he used the newspapers only to propagate his philosophy of truthfulness and non-violence. And for that purpose, his news values as understood by us would have greater relevance in the present day context.

4

Gandhiji and Development Journalism

I have taken up journalism not for its sake but merely as aid to what I have conceived to be my mission in life. My mission is to teach by example and precept under severe restraint the use of the matchless weapon of satyagraha which is a direct corollary of non-violence and truth... To be true to my faith, therefore, I may not write idly, I may not write merely to excite passion. The reader can have no idea of the restraint I have to exercise from week to week in the choice of topics and my vocabulary. It is training for me. It enables me to peep into myself and to make discoveries of my weaknesses. Often my vanity dictates a smart expression or my anger a harsh adjective. It is a terrible ordeal but fine exercise to remove these words.

—Gandhiji, *Young India*, July 2, 1925

Developmental journalism covers the entire gamut of socio-economic and cultural events, and it does not differ drastically from regular news coverage. Rather, its emphasis is more on developmental aspects keeping in view the context of development; and it examines critically and reports the relevance, enactment and impact of developmental programmes. Thus, Mahatma Gandhiji in India practiced development reporting even before the term, development journalism[1] came into existence. Mahatma Gandhiji, who was a development journalist, felt that the newspaper's role was to educate the masses, he profusely wrote on contemporary topics such as Hindu-Muslim unity, removal of untouchability, prohibition, promotion of *khadi* and other village industries, and the popularization of spinning wheel as a means of supplementing the income of the semi-starved and unemployed village peasants in India (Krishna Murthy, 1966: 79-80). During Independence, the Press was an effective medium in the hands of nationalists as well as social reform groups. They exposed social evils like casteism, child marriages, ban on remarriage of widows, social, legal, and other inequalities for which women were subjected. It also helped them in carrying out a massive campaign to educate the people on the eradication of untouchability (Krishna Murthy, 1966; Desai, 1993: 237; Yadava, 1985). Because, journalism in those days functioned as a mission to awaken the masses socially and politically (Yadava, 1985; Parthasarathy, 1991).

Thus Gandhiji set an example to the journalists in practicing development journalism with an intention to reform the society. He believed that the role of newspapers was only public service, and hence he wrote a series of stories on various issues such as health, birth control, and women upliftment and so on. For instance, he wrote a series of articles on birth control in *Young India* and *Harijan* beginning in 1925 as he was against the use of contraceptives to control the population. On April 4, 1925, he wrote: "If it is contended that birth-control is necessary for the nation because of over-population, I dispute the proposition. It has never been proved. In my opinion, by a proper land system, better agriculture and a supplementary industry, this country is capable of supporting twice as many people as they are in it today." On another occasion, he was candid in saying about women's problems of forcible use of contraceptives. He wrote in *Harijan* on May 2, 1936: "To ask India's women to take to contraceptives is to say the least, putting the cart before the horse. The first thing is to free her from mental slavery, to teach her the sacredness of her body, and to teach her the dignity of national service and the service of humanity." At the same time, he was a visionary though he denied it, and he foresaw the things that would happen in the coming decades. One trait of a development journalist is that he should signal the coming events before the people would understand the consequences of any action. Gandhiji as a development journalist continued to write about the birth control methods in *Harijan* on March 28, 1936. He said: "I know what havoc the secret vice has played among school boys and school girls. The introduction contraceptives under the name of science and the *imprimatur* of known leaders of society has intensified the complication and made the task of reformers who work for purity of social well-nigh impossible..." However, on an earlier occasion in *Young India* (April 10, 1930), he admonished men for degrading women. He said: To call woman the weaker sex is a libel; it's man's injustice to woman. If by strength is meant brute strength, then indeed is woman less brute than man. If by strength is meant moral power, then woman is immeasurably man's superior...If non-violence is the law of our being, the future is with woman. Further, in 1946, he advised women "not to look for men for protection. They must rely on their own strength and purity of character and on God" (*Harijan,* September 15, 1946).

About educating rural masses, Gandhiji wrote articles in *Harijan,* by giving the farming population rudimentary instructions about food. 'Milk and banana make a perfect meal,' he wrote in *Harijan* of February 15, 1935 in an article entitled 'Green Leaves and their Food Value'. "For nearly five months I have been living on uncooked foods. The addition of green leaves to their meals will enable villagers to avoid many diseases from which they are now suffering,' He devoted another article to the debate on 'Cow's Milk versus Buffalo's, and still a third to the supreme Indian problem: rice. In his booklet, *Key to Health,* and elsewhere, Gandhi gave warning against machine - polished rice. Polishing removes an overcoat rich in vitamins, especially B_1, he explained: lacking those vitamins, Indians, for most of whom rice is the chief staple food, are subject to numerous debilitating diseases, notably beriberi which means 'I cannot'. Hand-pounded rice, Gandhi explained, retains the vitamin - rich coating (Fischer, 1994: 407).

At other times, Gandhi explained about the nutritional value of the mango kernel and the groundnut or peanut. Gandhi knew that the improvement of seed, the proper use of fertilizer and the proper care of cattle could solve some of the basic problems of life. Gandhi also paid attention to non - agrarian aspects of village life. He wrote in *Harijan* on August 29, 1936 that 'we have to concentrate on the village being self contained, manufactured mainly for use'. 'Provided this character of village industry is maintained, there would be no objection to villagers using even the modern machines and tools that they can make and afford to use. Only they should not be used as a means of exploiting others.'

In *Harijan* of July 26, 1942 Gandhi described the ideal Indian village: "It is a complete republic, independent of its neighbours for its vital wants, and yet interdependent for many other wants in which dependence is necessity. Thus every village's first concern will be to grow its own food crops and cotton for its cloth. It should have a reserve for its cattle, recreation and playground for adults and children. Then if there is more land available, it will grow useful money crops, thus excluding ....tobacco, opium, and the like. The village will maintain a village theatre, school and public hall. It will have its own water works ensuring clean supply. This can be done through controlled wells and tanks (reservoirs). Education will be compulsory up to the final basic course. As far as possible, every activity will be conducted on a cooperative basis.' To this modest blueprint, which, however, seemed like a sketch of heaven to India's permanently underfed farmers, Gandhi added another wild dream: electricity in every village home (Fischer, 1994).

Gandhiji as a development journalist showed an example to the present day newspapers how to practice development journalism. Further, after Independence, that mission was partly carried by researchers as well as newspapers in conducting a few experiments in development journalism to accelerate rural development. Selden Menefee and Audrey Menefee conducted an interesting study of mimeographed newspaper in Mysore containing some developmental information. Known as *Menefee experiment,* a small newspaper called *Gram Samachar* (village news) was published in Kannada, the local knowledge, for 13 weeks to test the effects of communication on the villagers. For the purpose, four villages were chosen near Mysore in Karnataka. The researchers found an increase in the information level of the regular readers because of the newspaper (Menefee and Menefee, 1967).

In 1969, B.G. Verghese, the then editor of The *Hindustan Times,* New Delhi proved that the development reporting would be helpful to accelerate development. Verghese asked a team of reporters to write periodically about *Chattera,* a small village in Haryana, about its people, their problems and the process of development taking in that village (Yadava, 1991). Aggarwal (1978b) reported: Our village, *Chattera....* is a bold attempt to give rural orientation to the predominantly urban based and elite-oriented newspapers in the country. It is the form of journalism that can prove of immense help in bridging the rural-urban communication gap in the Third World."

The Indian Press has taken up development-linked campaigns for the public good. The Press has a social responsibility function apart from educating, informing and entertaining the public. The theory of social responsibility postulates that the Press has to play a crucial role in the people-centric issues. Because people depend on newspapers for their day-to-day information needs, newspapers should act to inform and educate people on social issues. The socially responsible press helps the citizens to be well informed on issues of immediate concern to them (Murthy, 2001: 105). Moreover, the degree of media attention given to social and developmental issues makes people and government take necessary action on them. In this context, the Press in India played an activist role for effecting changes in development. A few case studies in development journalism are presented below to understand the role of newspapers in development.

Udayavani Experiment

Udayavani, a Kannada daily established in 1970 which is published from Manipal (Karnataka) carried a 3-year (1981-84) experiment in development journalism, 'Identify Backward Village Experiment' in early 1980s. In order to carry out the experiment, the newspaper carried an advertisement on January 2, 1981 detailing the objectives of the experiment by inviting nominations from the readers. The advertisement was as follows:

> Udayavani has taken up a novel scheme to identify a backward village for studying the impact of numerous Central and State Government-sponsored schemes since Independence. Readers' involvement is of paramount importance. They are encouraged to identify two backward villages, one in their *taluka* and one in the district. To help you, a proforma listing the ten basic infrastructure facilities has been provided. These facilities have been identified based on Government of India census report.

The newspaper identified a backward village if it does not have a primary school, middle school, electricity, post office, telephone, doctor, hospital, drinking water, road, and bus service. The newspaper encouraged readers to identify a backward village basing on the above criteria and a 50-day time limit was fixed to send their nominations. A total of 465 readers sent their nominations identifying 417 villages and hamlets in the district as backward. However, keeping in view the scope and nature of the experiment, nominations from eight *talukas* of the district were considered for further evaluations. The readers' responses were analyzed with a view to selecting the most backward villages. In the next stage, 15 legislators were involved in identifying the villages from the district and they selected 10 villages. Further, *taluka* level officials were asked to identify villages under their jurisdiction by checking their official records. The coordinator of the project, Sanjay Daitota, travelled over 1900 kms. to verify and crosscheck the information given by the people. At the end of

17-day visit, the coordinator could identify 10 backward villages for the experiment. The identified villages were: (1) Alanthaya (2) Bellapady (3) Bolmane (4) Didupe (5) Kemtoor (6) Kudyady (7) Malachowki (8) Mandekolu (9) Manila, and (10) Navoora.

The main problems of these villages were: non-availability of potable drinking water, mosquito menace, frequent malarial attacks, diarrhea, and other water-borne diseases. Since the villages lacked even a miniscule of medical facilities, the patients had to be taken to nearby towns for medicare. Lack of proper roads along with isolation of villages made the emergency medical care very difficult (Daitota and Sanjay, 1990: 8). To make the project successful, some youth in these villages were motivated to take up developmental works, and later these youth formed a team of grassroot reporters for the newspaper. The newspaper decided to highlight the problems and to sensitize the people for solving their problems. In the first year, the newspaper covered all the problems and activities of the villages extensively and regularly. The coverage concentrated on developmental processes with an interpretation of the problems when the coordinator was touring the villages to understand the village's problems. In the second year, the coverage was restricted to happenings and occasional success stories. In the third year, there was no coverage of any issue while the coordinator was contacting the youth who were working as field assistants.

Moreover, the coverage concentrated on ordinary folks instead of politicians and rural elite. For instance, Maila, a resident of Mandekolu village was the first to travel by a bus to the village could easily be recognized in the village after a photo story on him appeared in the newspaper. The coverage used all formats of publications such as front-page news, photo-features, readers' complaints and double-page supplements. The coverage accelerated the process of development in South Karnataka. Farm clinics and school library came into existence. Officials cooperated with the villagers and youth and others participated in developmental works.

In another experiment, a researcher started a rural newspaper, *Gramyavani*, in 1993 in Deulpudi, a village in Ganjam district of Orissa to give information to the rural people. The fortnightly newspaper reaching eight villages of the *panchayat* continued for 16 months. A major objective of the newspaper was to provide development-linked information to the people. The contents of the newspaper included agriculture, health, forestry, and animal husbandry. The newspaper brought awareness among the villagers exposed to the newspaper (Jena, 1995). The two studies proved that the newspapers could raise the information level of the people and thereby contribute to accelerating developmental processes at the individual and societal level.

Campaign on Drugs

In early 1990s, *Indian Express* campaigned against drug peddling and its affects on youth, government servants, police constables and so on in Delhi and its surrounding areas. The campaign started on July 15, 1994 and ended on August 18, 1994. The paper published a series of stories filed by two reporters, Ajay Suri *and* Sanjiv Sinha. The July 15 story headlined as 'Dope against hope with a *pudiya* of smack in hand' appeared on the front-page.

> New Delhi-No less than three lakh people find themselves at the gateway to hell. For these flower children of the 70s, who have blossomed into confirmed heroin addicts, there is no hope at all. Every morning, every evening, they snort, sniff and smoke themselves to death...If the sprawling *jhuggi* clusters, unauthorized colonies and resettlement dwellings of East Delhi now constitute the drug dealers heaven, there are at least 10 colonies on this side of the Yamuna where smack is there for the asking.

The July 16 story mainly focuses on the trafficking of drugs into the country's capital, with a headline: Delhi drug '*mandi*' rendezvous for traffickers and the intro says:

New Delhi: It is child's play to smuggle in drugs into the Capital. In this city of one crore, there are few points which can be plugged to stop the inflow of indigenous heroin and Golden Crescent consignments destined for the West. Delhi is the new bazaar, a happy hunting ground for the drug overlords. Police seem helpless in stemming the tide. The few who are nabbed usually small time peddlers go scot-free with weak cases being made out against them. The big fish continue to have a free reign, rarely falling into the police net.

Specifically, July 17 story blamed the police for the booming drug traffic with a headline, Delhi cops turn Nelson's eye to drug trade. A part of the front-page story says... the 105 police stations in Delhi, equally empowered to arrest traffickers, have their own reasons to shirk duty. If you cannot fight them, ignore them, or better still, join them. This appears to be the new police motto.

Subsequent stories described the drug consumption in some other states of the country. A three-part story beginning from July 25 highlighted the drug trafficking across the country. The newspaper covered drug smuggling in the North India, North-Eastern states and South India. The result of the campaign was the Narcotics Control Bureau officials raided the places (*Indian Express,* August 11, 1994). They arrested the people connected with the trade. Ultimately, it led to the development of a master plan to control drug trafficking in the country (*Indian Express,* August 18, 1994).

Troubled Hearts

Health upkeep is a serious concern for a common man and with the rising health disorders; the common man is at wits' ends to deal with the situation. State Governments spend money on hospitals, yet they lack infrastructure, making common man run for helter-skelter for help. *The New Indian*

Express in a 13-part series of stories on the state of hospitals in Andhra Pradesh investigated the reasons for the hospitals' failure to deliver healthcare to the people. The paper wrote on the focused theme, 'Troubled hearts' from October 6 to October 19, 2004. The October 6 headline, 'Andhra Pradesh's medical shame' had the big intro as follows:

> Every Friday and Tuesday, a shameful spectacle unfolds on the steps of the Gandhi Hospital in Hyderabad. Hundreds of parents bring their toddlers and wait for directions to a corporate hospital where the young ones get a fresh lease of life. Some have holes in their hearts, some have palpitations, and some children's hearts miss the rhythm. Most of the time they go back disheartened. The State Government, which gave them land on the cheap to these hospitals, pleads with them to treat the children for Rs. 50,000. The corporate hospitals say no. Charity organizations are passing the hat so that the children can get operated on.

The paper reports corruption is rampant in the hospitals coupled with funds' crunch to buy equipment. Combined with these problems, staff positions are vacant. The paper says that the shortage of funds, staff, security and infrastructure amenities has made a mockery of the State Government's oft-repeated assertions that it is committed to providing proper healthcare to the poor. Further, the newspaper reports present poignant tale of hospitals. The premier Gandhi Hospital in the state capital refers any patient to Osmania General Hospital for CT scan because CT scanner is not available in the Gandhi Hospital, and thereby prolonging the agony of the patient. When the patient goes to the Osmania Hospital, the state's biggest hospital runs out of film. The AP Medical Housing and Infrastructure Development Corporation supplies the film and officials take their own time in meeting such requirements. In fact, another big hospital in the state capital, NILOUFER Hospital for children and women present an inhuman face of doctors. The October 10 story writes:

> Hyderabad: Here the doctors declare a child dead although he is alive. The doctors even prepare a death certificate for the child though signs of life are found in the child. Because of such treatment, the National Human Rights Commission sought a report from the State Government about the state of affairs in the hospital.

When this is the prevailing situation in the hospitals in the state capital, it is another story in the hospitals located in the district headquarters. The October 12 story headlined, 'Filth to the fore at Guntur Hospital'. The following is the intro:

> Guntur: Walk into the Government General Hospital here and you may just mistake it for a market place. At least, 10,000 people visit the hospital daily. They eat, urinate, defecate, spit, and the hygiene is...well...here's an incident that says it all. Only recently, a two-day-old male baby died allegedly due to ant bites at the hospital's prenatal intensive care unit.

The story pinpoints a statement of the doctor in the Guntur Hospital: A woman doctor wonders how she can spend her remaining 12 years of service in the hospital. It is not patients, but the health of the doctors which is at peril, says she. "The October 13 story of Guntur Hospital presents a deeper side of the malady." Low salary and petty politics are taking heavy toll on some doctors in the Guntur Hospital. The result: Some seasoned doctors are seeking voluntary retirement while others are silently bearing with the hardship of meager salaries.

Contrary to Guntur Hospital, the King George Hospital, at Visakhapatnam tells a different story. Since doctors are less, patients are packed of in 2 or 3 minutes. The doctors admit that at least 10 to 15 minutes are needed for preliminary investigation. This is because of shortage of doctors. Added to it, equipment does not work or under repair. Much more than these hospitals, Ruia Hospital at Tirupathi reminds that is there any hospital to look after the health of the patients. Two reports on October 17 and October 18 about the hospital tell the story. The October 18 story had the headline, 'Pigs have free run of Ruia Hospital'. The intro of the story is:

> Tirupathi, October 17: Have you ever seen a piggery on the premises of a Government General Hospital? Not only pigs are reared here, but also they are auctioned once in a month. Chenchaih, a pig rearer from nearby Giripuram village has been running a piggery right in front of the psychiatry ward... and the piggery has strength of 26 and Chenchaih collects the left over food from the hostel mess and feeds the pigs...Even dogs can be seen all around the hospital and wards. Recently, a bitch delivered four puppies in the male medical ward I.

Do doctors have ethics? If so, do you find them sincere in their duty? The October 19 story on Kadapa General Hospital concludes with a headline, 'No medicine here for a dog bite'.

> Kadapa: When a dog bites a man in Kadapa, it is news. Because the government hospital has no anti-rabies vaccine and the patient gets a bandage and is sent home. Shocked? Don't be.

The doctors have nursing homes and shift the patients there. Though the government rules say that the doctors are not supposed to practice outside, they do, without any transfers. "It is an open secret. Bit I keep my eyes shut as a majority of the doctors have clout" said district coordinator of government hospital...

These reports speak volumes of the state of government hospitals and the reports exposed them. Probably prompted by these reports, the State Government sanctioned Rs. 8 crores for the welfare of cardiac children to undergo treatment in the hospitals. At least, the government is sensitive in this regard and the Press has played its role in development.

Ecological Mismanagement

The *tsunami* on December 26, 2004 left a trail of destruction in the Asian region, killing more than 1.5 lakh people. The three southern states, viz., Andhra Pradesh, Tamil Nadu and Kerala in India experienced the worst-ever tragedy. Prompted by the tragedy, the *New Indian Express* deputed three reporters to investigate the reasons for huge losses suffered by the people. Furthermore, the newspaper published five-part reports beginning from January 20, 2005 on the human greed, which mismanaged the ecology for many years. The January 20 report carried with a streamer on the front page, 'Sea of life, Sea of death'. The blurb stated:

> If there were mangrove plantations, if only there was a warning, if there was no sand quarrying, if the Coastal Regulation Zone laws were enforced...The list of ifs that could have prevented the December 26 death wave goes on. As our reporters fanned out across Andhra Pradesh coast they discovered the shocking tale of greed where mangroves were destroyed, violations of rules where aquaculture farms cropped near the high tide line and evidence of another disaster in the making.

The reports focused on the process of destruction along the coast by digging deep into the facts of official apathy and human ignorance. The essence of these five reports is presented for the benefit of readers to understand the height of human greed in destroying the ecology. The January 20 story focuses on the following:

> For the last 15 years, sea has been eating this shoreline village, Uppada, 15 km. off Kakinada town, which is a district headquarters of East Godavari. Two guesthouses of the *zilla parishad,* two school buildings, a couple of temples, a well laid out road and several hundred acres of land have been swallowed up by the sea. The people of this region live in perpetual fear of advancing sea. Uppada is not a stray case. All along

> the 1030-km. coastline in the state, the sea has been eating up the 2842 coastal villages inch by inch, endangering 75-lakh fisher folks.

That is the destruction in the coastline. The chief reason for this impending destruction is, mangroves act as the natural barriers from advancing cyclonic waves. Even in the latest *tsunami,* the areas where there was large-scale destruction of mangroves were the ones to suffer the greatest damage. When this is happening the government has remained complacent about it. The report on January 21 highlights the state of affairs.

> The green zone does not exist in the Konaseema area. Because the Union Government-enacted Coastal Regulation Zone Act to protect the environmental degradation of the coast, it was never translated into action. Along the coast, the government had prohibited setting up of aqua ponds within 15km. of the tidal bank canals; there are aqua ponds all along the coast, violating the Act.

As the government is planning to encourage tourism, the CRZ Act is violated. The government is keen on augmenting its revenue; it is permitting setting up of cottages to attract more number of tourists. The January 22 report reveals the opinion of the experts.

> A team of Geological Survey of India experts who conducted studies along the coast in the post-*tsunami* from December 29, 2004 to January 6, 2005 also felt that the coastline land pattern was getting affected. The team members said that beach tourism could be one of the reasons for the degradation of the coastline.

Along the coastline, government encouraged aquaculture farms and people invested money on building up the farms. Although the farms did not yield any considerable gains to the people in terms of income, the ground water levels were destroyed. The January 23 report specifically focused on this aspect of ecological destruction.

> ...mushrooming aquaculture ponds along these areas has adversely impacted the ground water salinity. Due to high water salinity levels, migration from this area (Prakasam district) has increased. According to a survey by the Rural Water Supply Department, the salinity which was 3 parts per million (ppm), a couple of years ago, has shot up to an alarming 12.3 ppm making the water non-usable.

Is there any solution to this problem? Can the government redeem the loss on account of its failure to check the malaise? The reports evoked response from the government and January 24 report focused on the government's plan to grow plants along the coast.

> The State Government is planning a massive afforestation drive along the 1032km. coastline at a cost of Rs. 500 crore to take sting out of any *tsunami* or tidal wave. A five-year timeframe has been fixed for the project.

The five-part story impacted the Central Government, which asked the Chennai-based Dr. M.S. Swami Nathan Foundation to conduct a study on coastal belt forestry in all states. In essence, it can be inferred that the process reporting in development journalism will induce development thinking in the policy makers and the government.

Campaign for Prohibition

Newspapers can advocate for a cause and *Eenadu*, the largest circulated Telugu daily in Andhra Pradesh proved it by supporting anti-arrack movement launched in the State in 1992. Adult literacy classes for women had impacted most of the rural women and Rosamma, a woman in Dubagunta Village in Nellore district launched a struggle for banning liquor. Inspired by a story, *Seethamma katha* taught in the classroom textbook, Rosamma started a movement for banning liquor. *Eenadu*, on March 8, 1993, published an account of the movement.

The real story began in May 1992 at Dubagunta, a village in Nellore, when three drunkard labourers lost their way and were drowned in the village tank. The women of the village marched to the arrack shop and forced its closure. Obviously, *Seethamma katha,* an important lesson that they learnt in the adult literacy class, was at the back of their minds (cited in Jeffrey, 2003: 14).

Soon, the movement spread all over the state and the supporters attacked liquor shops and burnt down the manufacturing units. In 1993, the newspaper devoted a full page to prohibition, "War on Liquor", proclaimed a headline in the paper on February 22, 1993. The paper continuously supported the movement from April 15, 1992 to April 16, 1993. During the movement, the paper highlighted various news items related to the movement such as writing background stories, reviewing the progress of the movement, discussing the ill-effects of liquor consumption and holding meetings with a cross section of the population (Anita, 2008). The newspaper published full-page news, features, editorial cartoons and other stories along with a pocket cartoon everyday on the movement while publishing a pocket cartoon on the front page daily for more than one year. Because of the newspaper campaign and support to the movement, the State Government declared prohibition in the state in 1994.

Conservation of Water

The Andhra Pradesh Government launched water conservation programme in 2000 appealing to the residents to conserve water. *Eenadu,* the largest circulated daily in the State launched a water conservation programme in support of the governments programme. The reason for taking up this campaign was that the paper set an agenda for itself. On May 7, 2000, chief editor of the paper, Ramaji Rao in a signed editorial published on the front page declared the policy of the paper:

> ...Drought is spreading its tentacles all over the state and the dipping water levels are increasingly affecting

> the people and agriculture. Lackadaisical attitude of the people coupled with the administrative apathy towards recharging water sources led to the present crisis. Unless people come together to fight the vagaries of Nature, the state cannot surmount the impending crisis. Regardless of political parties and people's affiliations to different political ideologies, all must take up repairing works to the age-old water tanks and wells...About 29 countries across the globe are suffering from severe water crisis. To utter dismay of everyone in the world, every Andhra man or woman must take part in the "great ritual of water harvesting." About 30,000 villages in the State have to prepare the water tanks and wells to retain every drop of water that seeps into the earth during the rainy season. In the coming 40 days, the rainy season will begin and everyone must keep the water pits to absorb rainwater. In this great ritual, *Eenadu* along with its television channel, ETV will support the movement by highlighting the success stories of the villages. The newspaper will publish opinions of experts for the benefit of the readers. The paper on recognizing the success of the village in implementing the programme will felicitate the village by giving a prize. The paper is behind you for performing the great ritual.

The coverage was positive for the programme *Neeru-Meeru*. *Eenadu* in all its 23 editions allocated a full page with the title, *Sujalam-Suphalam* to create awareness about water harvesting among people. Slogans, offbeat photos, messages from intellectuals and details from experts were published in the page. The paper declared a policy that everyyear the paper starts the awareness programme from April to June 10 by publishing a full page on water conservation (Murthy, 2006).

As seen in these case studies, development-related issues appeared in the newspaper when a crisis or an issue hit the country. However, the growth of print media has been a phenomenon in the last five years in the country with the increase in circulation or readership. With the increase in the reach of the newspapers, the invention of technology and also the growth of literacy have helped the newspaper industry in the country. Because of these reasons, the press can report more stories on development which will benefit the majority of the people in rural areas. Nevertheless, the newspaper space given to development news does not exceed even five per cent of the newshole (Murthy, 2001).

NOTE

In 1967, with the coinage of the term, development journalism by Alan Chalkley, it gained popularity with the creation of Press Foundation of Asia, financed jointly by Asian Newspapers and Ford Foundation (Altshull, 1984: 151). Nevertheless, those who conceived development journalism in the beginning believed that national development depended heavily on economic development and felt that journalists trained in economics could report competently about problems pertaining to a developing nation. Therefore, Alan Chalkley's book, published in 1968, *The Manual of Development Journalism* which laid emphasis on economics and it suggested training for journalists in economic reporting. According to Chalkley (1968), the purpose of development journalism was to inform and give readers the facts and a development journalist was expected to use simple terms and to avoid jargon. Further, when the concept was gaining currency, different experts offered various definitions to development journalism. Vilanilam (1975) defined development journalism as journalism that deals with the process of development in developing nations. Aggarwal (1978a) pointed out that development journalism in brief is the reporting of development process rather than events. The emphasis in development news is not what happens at a particular moment or on a given day but what is happening over a period of time. Development news covers the entire gamut of socio-economic and cultural development-even non-development problems as well as prospects. Further, Aggarwal (1978b) explained that development news in its treatment is not different from regular news or investigative reporting. It can deal with development issues at the macro and micro levels and can take different forms at national and international levels. In covering the development news beat, a journalist should critically examine, evaluate and report the relevance of a development project to national and local needs, the differences between its impacts on people as claimed by the government official and as it actually is. Ogan (1982), while agreeing with the Aggarwal, observed that development journalism means the critical examination and report of the relevance, enactment and impact of development programmes. Even the Second Press Commission (1982) noted, "Development reporting should tell the story of what is going well as well as what is going wrong. It should investigate the reasons for success as well as for failure, at different places under the different conditions, of various development programmes affecting the lives of common people." Contrary to these definitions, veteran journalist with leftist leanings Nikhil Chakravarty views development journalism in a different angle. Development journalism, according to Chakravarty (1983), embraces the magnificent story of the toiling man producing the wealth of the nation, on which he stakes his claim to be its master. Obviously, in presenting this fascinating drama, the media person has to be adequately equipped. And the basic equipment for this job is the faith in the common man, and the endeavour to be identified with his life so that the media may be able to articulate with sensitivity his moments of triumph and tribulations, his joys and sorrows. More specifically, Chakravarty understands development journalism from the Marxist perspective of the common man producing the wealth of the nation and he holds the means of production. Whatever may be the definitions, the aim of development journalism is to accelerate the processes of development to bring in remarkable change in the quality of life of majority of the people.

5

Conclusion

The press is called the fourth estate. It is definitely a power but to misuse that power is criminal. I am a journalist myself and would appeal to fellow journalists to realize their responsibility and to carry on their work with no idea other than that of upholding the truth.

—Gandhiji, *Harijan*, April 27, 1947

Is Gandhian journalism which emerged nearly a century back relevant today? During this century, Gandhiji showed to the world that his practice of non-violence, and strong determination to achieve his goals in the face of stiff resistance proved to be successful. Also in relation to journalism, his news values as discussed in Chapter II are highly relevant. Culture as a news value can be relevant even today in the wake of proliferation of newspapers and news channels. With the continuous of supply of news or events by alien channels in the form of entertainment, it is argued that the channels impact the culture of a country, and in the arena of international communication, it is described as cultural imperialism.[1] Obviously, these news channels promote consumer culture with an intention to dominate the markets with their goods. Thus, Gandhiji aptly described these consumer goods as bodily comforts which provide the well being of the individual physically while distancing her/him from culture of the country. An observation of newspaper or television contents reveal that civilization as described by Gandhiji is taking deep roots. Gandhiji said in *Young India* on June 1, 1921

> I do not want my house to be walled in all sides and my windows to be stuffed. I want the cultures of all lands to be blown about my house as freely as possible. But I refuse to be blown off my feet by any. I refuse in other people's houses as an interloper, a beggar or a slave. I refuse to put the necessary strain of learning English upon my sisters for the sake of false pride or questionable social advantage.

In fact, the argument to halt cultural imperialism of the West began in the early 1970s when the UNESCO set up a commission to study the mass media content at the instance of the Third World countries. Diplomats like Mustapha Masmoudi[2] (1979) Tunisian ambassador and permanent delegate to UNESCO and journalists like D.R. Mankekar (1978, 1981) in India raised their voice through mass media programmes to make the native culture insular from the external influences.

The second aspect of the Gandhian news values is peace. Peace as a news value is increasingly becoming relevant in the beginning of the 21st century. As defined by Gandhiji, non-violence is a conscious attempt to detach oneself from violence in spite of having strength and prowess. Thus, the emergence of peace journalism as suggested by Johan Galtung (2006) has greater relevance today. The mightiest personality in the 20th century, Gandhiji showed to the world the need to practice non-violence. It was observed that 'over times peace journalism could help society at large think and speak about non-violence and creativity when dealing with conflicts' (McGoldrick, and Lynch, 2000). Peace journalism favours the use of neutral and positive words in the news reports to inculcate good values among the readers. For instance, a study of headlines in *The Hindu* (p. 12) on February 2, 2009 showcased the low level of societal norms.

- Congress: report constitutionally erroneous

- How Chief Election Commissioner pursued BJP allegations
- Minister slams bribery in judiciary Nobody has power to get case registered against a sitting judge, he says
- Centre must accept CEC's advice: BJP
- Apex court to hear SEBI plea today
- CEC does not have *suo motu* power: Nariman
- "Ensure safe passage for civilians in Sri Lanka"
- Kalyan factor won't erode Muslim vote bank: Mulayam
- ED moves court on Satyam

A careful study of these headlines reveals the use of the words: 'erroneous', 'allegations', 'bribery in judiciary' 'SEBI plea in court' 'Muslim vote bank' and others. In another newspaper, even harsh and violent words have been used in the editorial. For instance, *Indian Express* editorial (February 2, 2009) contains the following:

It's about Tamils, not the Tigers

> The latest bout of **breast-beating and fist shaking** that is going on over the fate of Sri Lanka's Tamils, now that the Liberation Tigers of Tamil Eelam are penned into a tiny enclave in the north of the island, is a case of too little, too late. It may seem unfeeling not to join the state of shocked mourning that seems to have broken out suddenly all over Tamil Nadu, but the Sri Lankan army's steady, inexorable progress in the war against the LTTE was never a secret.

The use of negative words bribery, allegations, and plea in the court reflects the state of the society as media is said to be a mirror of society. Such words depict the negative meaning in the minds of newspaper readers, and the Gandhian journalism abhors the use of such words. Even the editorial which is supposed to be balanced and free from bias is increasingly becoming partisan.

Although, the third news value, development is always relevant in the country, developmental reporting has not gained much currency among Indian newspapers. Hence, vital issues such as primary education, population control, the state of urban decay, power crises, etc. get a backseat (Rai, 1992; Singh, 1994; Shourie, 1995). Further, reporting on rural development does not receive much importance in the Press although 70 per cent of the population in India lives in rural areas. Rural stories rarely get front-page coverage unless they are disastrous events such as starvation deaths, flood, famine or a policy pronouncement (Gupta, 1994). Gandhiji was insisting that *purna swaraj* was possible only when all the villages were developed. Because development is a very wide subject and it is a long-drawn process, and therefore two types of reporting emerge in relation to the treatment of development news. In two types of reporting—process and events—the trend in newspapers is to focus on events instead of process. Since development is a process, it requires a constant study and comprehension of the subjects. In journalism, journalists are keen on reporting events. Nearly three decades back, the Second Press Commission (1982) observed: "The reporting of non-official initiatives in rural development, educational reforms, leprosy eradication and so on is less extensive than the in-depth reporting of the implementation of official development programmes. It is unfortunate that our newspapers become aware of such non-official activities only after they have been honoured by Jamanalal Bajaj foundation or Magsasay award."

The post-Independence period of the Indian Press has witnessed radical changes, and its mission has completely taken a different turn. Noted journalist G.S. Bhargava (2005: 103) said that 'the transformation of the press from a mission to service and ultimately to industry and the consequent conversion of journalists from upholders of values and causes to industrial wage earners had a profound effect on the quality and character of the profession'. In terms of contents, the Indian newspapers fall into two categories: elite and sensational papers as contents or rather news in newspapers play a key role in judging the character of the paper. Elite newspapers focus on serious issues while sensational papers are keen on trivial issues. Rather, the difference in the Indian Press is slowly fading between the two categories (Murthy, 2005: 42). Circulation is oxygen for the survival of the newspaper, and the papers adopt new strategies. Principally, news is made to attract the large sections of the readers. On this count, the elite papers too adopt the same strategies being adopted by the sensational papers. The chief reason for this trend is commercialization of the press on account of the entry of businessmen into the profession of journalism. Veteran journalist Chalapati Rao (1982) observed that 'the broad feature of the Indian Press is that it is an industry, which is owned and managed by other industries'. Further, he commented, "The working class, the poor peasant, the lawless labour, does not exist for mass media. We are hopelessly witnessing the rapid growth of the big business press and the government."

As commercialization has set in, the newspapers focus on contents that attract the attention of the readers. Obviously, the Indian Press is known for its wide coverage of political news (Murthy, 2000), gossip (Sainath, 1996: 436) and sensationalism (Goswami, 1994). Political news is given a prominent place in all the newspapers, irrespective of language. In a study conducted by Murthy (2000), it was found that political news ranked the highest in the selected English and regional newspapers. On the front page, two themes politics, and crime, moral problems occupy three-fourths of the space. Because the front page is the most significant page, newspapers focus on political and sensational events to grab the readers' attention.

Obviously, the vicissitudes of the political parties, mudslinging and allegations against each other form the grist to the reporters' mill. News stories on crime and moral problems also get considerable attention on the front page. Stories on theft, burglary, cheating, and law and order problems appear more frequently on the front page. Such issues contain news values that enable papers to boost circulation.

Pritish Nandy (1994a) aptly observed: Issues like poverty, homelessness, and unemployment are no longer on the front page. What you have, instead, is the odd sex and violence story to keep the flag of investigative journalism flying. The former editor of *Times of India* Sham Lal (2003: 313) succinctly observed that 'in the world of rat race, pop culture, sales talk, and seductive images, there is no space for a somber analysis of complex issues. A well-argued point is more likely to tire out the viewers than puerile asides by a pop star or a political big shot'.

Public controversies surrounding politicians or celebrities are also sensationalized. Chalapati Rao (1982) observed that the present day newspapers, which seek to be popular by trying to be sensational, are practicing the cult of personality in the crudest possible form. Of late, the private issues of public personalities get front-page treatment.

Slowly, the definition of news that is taught in the journalism classrooms is radically changing. The newspapers have their own definitions of news. The popular dailies define news differently from the traditional definitions of news. The old definition of news concentrates on public interest, which is modified in the present day context as news with a public personality in the focus (Murthy, 2004: 29). Therefore, the priorities of news are changing. Pritish Nandy (1994b), the former editor of the *Illustrated Weekly of India,* wrote:

> What about quality journalism? Changing the world for the better? Frankly, who cares about it? Entertainment is the opiate of the masses today and journalists are busy competing with their own advertising departments to bring you leisure-led marketing vehicles that celebrate designer trash. Be it magazines or TV shows or even newspapers and colour offerings, they are all falling over each other to showcase the talent less and trivial. The packaging is skilful and the content is zilch.

Flimsy and non-relevant issues get more space in the newspapers. Ninan (2003) observed that the trend in 1970s was news editors frowned if a company name was mentioned in the copy. Because, public was more worthy than private, politics more worthy than business and governance more worthy than entertainment. Contrary to the earlier trend, in the present day journalism, news about personalities is salient, and it's personal journalism instead of public journalism. Newspapers compete with television channels in covering the glamour. Executive editor of *India Today,* Kaveree Bamzai (2009), made a cryptic comment: "Unfortunately the accent is so much on glamour and on who is a celebrity and who's not. I think the whole notion of achievement has become diluted. There is a celebrity culture obsession where a Rakhi Sawant or a Mika are more popular than say someone who has brought electricity to a village or brought IT to a village... I suppose if you are a woman, you are expected to be glamorous and success is measured that way, so that gets accentuated."

Therefore, Nandy (1994a) again observes that 'colour sections zero in on designers, jewellery, lifestyle, stories, and promotions masquerading as editorial. Comics, crosswords and features sponsored by companies provide "intellectual breaks." The profession is changing. Squires (1990), a senior American journalist calls journalists as 'social entertainers'. Thus Sham Lal (2003: 314) felt that the quality of entertainment was declining. He observed that "the large the audience the lower the level not only of news coverage and comment but also of the quality of entertainment." He also pointed out that 'news has to be personalized. The copy has to be more snappy. The comment has to be brief and bursue so as not to fag out the reader or the viewer. And the packaging of the newspaper as well as the programme has to be more stylish. It is no accident that no television channel in India today has any place for classical music.'

Newspapers lack in-depth study or research on subjects relating to the nation. Events are more important than issues. Shourie (1995) points out that 'lack of specialization is a running sore of the Indian Press- whether it is on defence or on power projects, on the size of dams or on the virtues or otherwise of atomic power, there are very few journalists who have worked at studying the subject in any detail'. Karlekar, (2007) commented with concern:

> ...There is an increasing trend towards trivialization underlined by the attention paid to a strange category called Page Three people, to the lives and deeds of sports and film stars, successful captains of industry and business. Serious coverage, particularly that of the plight of the victims of globalization and forcible land acquisition to make room for special economic zones, mega industrial and infrastructural projects and townships, find little space. Nor does one find in the Indian media the kind of debate on globalization and the emergence of the market economy that one should. Clearly, the Indian media is fast absorbing the bland ethos of the globalized media. Ethics? Where is the place for such a thing in the globalized marketplace celebrating social Darwinism?

The chief reasons for not taking up development journalism by newspapers, according to Bhattacharjee (1994), are:

- Inadequate information and poor understanding of the subject of development among practicing journalists;
- Absence of training in marshalling and presenting of facts in an attractive format;
- Poor interest shown by newspapers in development coverage; and
- Lack of funds and support from the newspaper establishments.

Why are these news contents found predominantly in the newspapers? The newspapers argue that their sustenance depends on circulation and consequent advertising, and hence they focus on these contents to increase their circulation. Is their argument tenable? In a country like India, which is plagued with problems like illiteracy, lack of health care facilities, pollution, corruption, and the apathy of government officials etc., the role of the Press in development is desirable. Hence Gandhian journalism is highly relevant to a great extent in the context of development.

In respect of ethics, Gandhian journalism needs to be looked closely as it has great relevance even today. The Gandhian trait of positive journalism has radically undergone a change. For instance, Gandhiji observed that the British judges' consideration of contempt of court was praised by him. He admitted the "reprimand" given by judges was acceptable. He truthfully published it in the newspaper, and yet he defended himself. But, the modern newspapers don't even publish the Press Council of India reprimand or censure to the newspapers for violation of journalistic ethics. Courage of conviction and truth telling are the bedrock of the journalism profession. The foundations of Indian Press as laid by Mahatma Gandhiji are receding to the background in the present day owing to media's slow adoption of the western model of journalism, tabloidization which emphasizes on sensationalism, sex, and surprises. News reports are biased and personal involvement of journalists is quite discernible in the newspapers. Vilanilam (2005: 89) observed:

> "...The old Journalism of the Gandhian era, of journalists with noble goals, motivated by the need for social change in India, has disappeared, yielding to the journalism of the pocket book, of the purse in short-of pure greed. Journalism as service to society has been replaced by journalism aimed at profit and affluence for media promoters and media workers."

Therefore, Gandhian journalism has relevance even today, and journalists in the media establishments must bear them in mind when they are working. In view of the prevailing environment, the media in India must retrospect its' role in society in light of Gandhian journalism. When the newspapers fail to live up to the expectations of readers, Gandhiji while expressing his concern advised:

> Unfortunately, the newspapers have become more important to the average man than the scriptures. I

would fain advise them to give up reading newspapers. They would lose nothing by so doing whereas real food for their minds and spirits lies in the scriptures and other good literature (*Harijan*, April 27, 1947).

NOTES

1. Cultural imperialism thesis holds that dominant societies are able to impose their culture on that of subordinate societies as a means of establishing and perpetuating control. This is seen as part of the historical development of a wider economic and political imperialism illustrated particularly in the relationship between developed and under developed nations. More specifically, cultural imperialism refers to the speed of cultural values, ideas and practices which reflect and reproduce the 'superiority' of the dominant culture. At the same time it describes the devaluation and destruction of indigenous culture. (Casey *et al.*, 2002).

2. The argument for the New World Information and Communication Order (NWICO) was pioneered by Mustapha Masmoudi, the Tunisia's ambassador and permanent delegate to UNESCO. Masmoudi (1979) pointed out that the information in the modern world is characterized by basic imbalances, reflecting the general imbalance that affects the international community in three fields - political, legal and technico-financial. Specifically his arguments in the political sphere are relevant in the present context. They are:

   (1) **A flagrant quantitative imbalance between North and South.** Almost 80 per cent of the world news flow emanates from the major transnational agencies and out of this news flow, 20 to 30 per cent is devoted to the developing countries. (2) **An inequality in information resources.** The five major transnational agencies (AP, AFP, Reuter, UPI and TASS-ITAR) monopolize the news, while almost a Third of the developing countries do not possess a single national news agency. Inequality also exists in the distribution of the radio frequency spectrum between developed and developing countries. (3) **A de facto hegemony and a will to dominate.** With their domination of information, these agencies are indifferent to the problems of the Third World, and in turn, make them consume the information as a commodity. (4) **A lack of information on developing countries.** These western channels of information depict the Third World countries as strife-ridden, suffering from crises, strikes, street demonstrations. (5) **Survival**

of the colonial era. The present day information system perpetuates political, economic, and cultural colonialism. Information about the Third World is distorted in consonance with the interests of the transnational system. (6) **An alienating influence in the economic, social and cultural spheres.** In addition to dominating and manipulating the international news flow, the developed countries practice other forms of hegemony over the communications institutions of the Third World viz., ownership of media institutions in the Third World, near-monopoly of advertising and using them for propaganda. (7) **Messages ill-suited to the areas in which they are disseminated.** Even important news of the Third World is neglected in favour of other information of interest to build up public opinion of their respective countries.

Appendix

(Gandhiji gave the following written statement in connection with sedition case in 1922)

I owe it perhaps to the Indian public and to the public in England, to placate which this prosecution is mainly taken up that I should explain why from a staunch loyalist and cooperator, I have become an uncompromising disaffectionist and non-cooperator. To the court too I should say why I plead guilty to the charge of promoting disaffection towards the Government established by law in India.

My public life began in 1893 in South Africa in troubled weather. My first contact with British authority in that country was not of a happy character. I discovered that as a man and an Indian, I had no rights. More correctly I discovered that I had no rights as a man because I was an Indian.

But I was not baffled. I thought that this treatment of Indians was an excrescence upon a system that was intrinsically and mainly good. I gave the Government my voluntary and hearty cooperation, criticizing it freely where I felt it was faulty but never wishing its destruction.

Consequently when the existence of the empire was threatened in 1899 by the Boer Challenge, I offered my services to it, raised a volunteer ambulance corps and served at several actions that took place for the relief of Ladysmith. Similarly in 1906, at the time of the Zulu 'revolt', I raised a stretcher bearer party and served till the end of the 'rebellion'. On both the occasions I received medals and was even mentioned in dispatches. For my work in South Africa I was given by Lord Hardinge a Kaisar-i-Hind gold medal. When the war broke out in 1914 between England and Germany, I raised a volunteer ambulance corps in London, consisting of the then resident Indians in London, chiefly students. Its work was acknowledged by the authorities to be valuable. Lastly, in India when a special appeal was made at the War Conference in Delhi in 1918 by Lord Chelmsford for recruits, I struggled at the cost of my health to raise a corps in Kheda, and the response was being made when the hostilities ceased and orders were received that no more recruits were wanted. In all these efforts at service, I was actuated by the belief that it was possible by such services to gain a status of full equality in the empire for my countrymen.

The first shock came in the shape of the Rowlett Act- law designed to rob the people of all real freedom. I felt called upon to lead an intensive agitation against it. Then followed the Punjab horrors beginning with the massacre at Jallianwalabagh and culminating in crawling orders, public floggings and other indescribable humiliations. I discovered too that the plighted word of the Prime Minister to the Musalmans of India regarding the integrity of Turkey and the holy places of Islam was not likely to be fulfilled. But in spite of the forebodings and the grave warnings of friend, at the Amritsar Congress in 1919, I fought for cooperation and working of the Montague Chelmsford reforms, hoping that the Prime Minister would redeem his promise to the Indian Musalmans, that the Punjab wound would be healed, and that the reforms, inadequate and unsatisfactory though they were, marked a new era of hope in the life of India.

But all that hope was shattered. The Khilafat promise was not to be redeemed. The Punjab crime was whitewashed and most culprits went not only unpunished but reminded in service, and some continued to draw pensions from the Indian revenue and in some cases were even rewarded. I saw too that not only did the reforms not mark a change of heart, but they were only a method of further draining India of her wealth and of prolonging her servitude.

I came reluctantly to the conclusion that the British connection had made India more helpless than she ever was before, politically and economically. A disarmed India has no power of resistance against ant aggressor if she wanted to engage, in an armed conflict with him. So much is this the case that some of our best men consider that India must take generations, before she can achieve Dominion status. She has become so poor that she has little power of resisting famines. Before the British advent India spun and wove in her millions of cottages, just the supplement she needed for adding to her meager agricultural resources. This cottage industry, so vital for India's existence, has been ruined by incredibly heartless and inhuman processes as described by English witnesses. Little do town dwellers know how the semi starved masses of India are slowly sinking to lifelessness? Little do they know that their miserable comfort represents the brokerage they get for their worked theory of their foreign exploiter, that the profits and the brokerage are sucked from the masses? Little do they realize that the Government established by law in British India is carried on for this exploitation of the masses? No, sophistry, no jugglery in figures, can explain away the evidence that the skeleton in many villages present to the naked eye. I have no doubt whatsoever that both England and the town dwellers of India will have to answer, if there is a God above, for this crime against humanity, which is perhaps unequalled in history. The law itself in this country has been used to serve the foreign exploiter. My unbiased examination of the Punjab Martial Law cases has led me to believe that at least ninety-five per cent of convictions were wholly bed. My experience of political case in India leads me to the conclusion, in nine out of every ten, the condemned men were totally innocent. Their crime consisted in the love of their country. In ninety-nine cases out of hundred, Justice has been denied to Indian as against European in the courts of India. This is not an exaggerated picture. It is the experience of almost every

Indian who has had anything to do with such cases. In my opinion, the administration of the law is thus prostituted, consciously or unconsciously, for the benefit of the exploiter.

The greater misfortune is that the Englishmen and their Indian Associates in the administration of the country do not know that they are engaged in the crime I have attempted to describe. I am satisfied that many Englishmen and Indian officials honestly believe that they are administering one of the busy systems devised in the world, and that India is making steady, though, slow progress. They do not know a subtle but effective system of terrorism and an organized display of force on the one hand, and the deprivation of all powers of retaliation or self defence on the other, has emasculated the people and induced in them the habit of simulation. This awful habit has added to the ignorance and the self deception of the administrators. Section 124A, under which I am happily charged, is perhaps the prince among the political sections of the Indian Penal Code designated to suppress the liberty of the citizen. Affection cannot be manufactured or regulated by law. If one has no affection for a person or system, one should be free to give the fullest expression to his disaffection, so long as he does not contemplate, promote or incite to violence. But the section under which Mr. Banker and I are charged is one under which mere promotion of disaffection is crime. I have studied some of the cases tried under it: I know that some of the most loved of India patriots have been convicted under it. I consider it a privilege, therefore, to be charged under that section. I have endeavoured to give in their briefest outline the reasons for my disaffection. I have no personal ill will against any single administrator; much less can I have any disaffection towards the king's person. But, I hold it to be a virtue to be disaffected towards a government which in its totality has done more harm to India than any previous system. India is less manly under the British rule than she ever was before. Holding such a belief, I consider it to be a sin to have affection for the system. And it has been a precious privilege for me to be able to write what I have in the various articles tendered in evidence against me.

In fact, I believe that I have rendered a service to India and England by showing in non-cooperation the way out of the unnatural state in which both are living. In my opinion, non-cooperation with evil is as much a duty as is cooperation with good. But in the past, non-cooperation has been deliberately expressed in violence to the evil doer. I am endeavouring to show to my countrymen that violent non-cooperation only multiplies evil, and that as evil can only be sustained by violence, withdrawal of support of evil requires complete abstention from violence. Non-violence implies voluntary submission to the penalty for non-cooperation with evil. I am here, therefore, to invite and submit cheerfully to the highest penalty that can be inflicted upon me for what in law is deliberate crime, and what appears to me to be the highest duty of a citizen. The only course open to you, the judge and the assessors, is either to resign your posts and thus dissociate yourselves from evil, if you feel that the law you are called upon to administer is an evil, and that in reality I am innocent, or to inflict on me the severest penalty, if you believe that the system and the law you are assisting to administer are good for the people of this country, and that my activity is, therefore, injurious to the common weal.

(From Selected Works of Mahatma Gandhiji, Vol. VI, 1994, pp. 18-24)

Bibliography

•

Aggarwal, N. (1978a). 'Humanizing International News', *Media Asia,* 5(3):136-138.

Aggarwal, N. (1978b). 'A Third World Perspective of News'. *Freedom at Issue.* May-June.

Altshull, J.H. (1984). *Agents of Power: The Role of the News Media in Human Affairs,* New York: Longman.

Anita, G. (2008). 'Newspapers and Campaigns: A study of Eenadu's Coverage of Anti-Arrack Movement'. In DVR Murthy (ed.), *Media Research: Themes and Applications* (pp. 53-79). New Delhi: Kanishka Publishers.

Bagdikian, B. (1987). *Media Monopoly* (Second edition). Boston: Beacon Press.

Bamzai, Kaveree (2009, February 13). 'Is Indian media unfair to women achievers?'*Campaign India, Vol. II* (2), p. 7.

Bhargava, G.S. (2005). *The Press in India: An Overview,* New Delhi: National Book Trust.

Bhattacharjea, Arun (1994). 'The Constraints of Development Reporting' in M.R. Dua and V.S. Gupta (eds.), *Media and Development* (pp. 46-53), New Delhi: Har Anand.

Bhattacharya, B. (2002). *Gandhi, the Writer* (First reprint). New Delhi: National Book Trust.

Boyer J.H. (1981). 'How Editors View Objectivity?' *Journalism Quarterly*, 58 (1): 24-28.

Casey, B. Casey, N. Calvert, B. French, L. and Lewis, J. (2002). *Television Studies: The key studies*. London: Routledge.

Chakravarthy, N. (1983, April). 'Communicators Should Indicate the Direction of Development', *Communicator*, XVII (2).

Chalapathi Rao, M. (1982). 'Social Change and Unchanging Press', *Link*, August 15.

Chalkley, A. (1968). *A Manual of Development Journalism*, Manila: Thomson Foundation and Press Foundation of Asia.

Dalton, Dennis (1999). *Gandhi's Power: Non-violence in Action*, New Delhi: Oxford University Press.

Daitota, I. and Sanjay, B.P. (1990). *The Eighteenth Elephant: An Experiment in Development Journalism*, Manipal: Udayavani Press.

Dhar, A. (2009) 'A Silent Revolution', *The Hindu*, February 1, 2009.

Desai, A.R. (1993). *Social Background of Indian Nationalism* (Second Edition), Bombay: Popular Prakashan.

Fico, F. and Freedman, E. (2008).' Biasing Influences on Balance in Election News Coverage: An Assessment of Newspaper Coverage of the 2006 U. S. Senate Elections', *Journalism and Mass Communication Quarterly, 85*(3): 499-514.

Fischer, Louis (1994). *The Life of Mahatma Gandhiji* (Third impression). New Delhi: Harpar Collins Publishers India Pvt. Ltd.

Fowler, R. (1991). *Language in the News: Discourse and Identity in the Press*. London: Routledge.

Galtung, J. (2006, fall). 'Peace Journalism as an Ethical Challenge'. *Global Media Journal (Mediterranean Edition), 1(2): 1-5.*

Galtung, J. (1998, September 3-6), *Peace Journalism: What , Why, Who, How, When, Where.* Paper presented in the workshop, What are peace journalists for? TRANSCEND, Taplow Court, UK.

Gandhi, M.K. (2005). *Hind Swaraj or Indian Home Rule* (seventeenth reprint), Ahmedabad, Navajivan Trust.

Goswami, N. (1994). 'A Carnival of Clones', *Indian Express,* New Delhi, July 24.

Gupta, V.S. (1994). 'Constraints in Rural Reporting', in M.R. Dua and V.S. Gupta (eds.), Media and Development (pp. 39-45), New Delhi: HarAnand.

Hanitzsch, T. (2004). 'Journalists as Peacekeeping Force? Peace Journalism and Mass Communication Theory', *Journalism Studies,* 5(4), 483-495.

Harcup, T. and O'Neill, D. (2001). 'What is News? Galtung and Ruge Revisited'. *Journalism Studies, 2(2)*: 261-80.

Hay, Stephen (2002). 'Gandhiji: Guide to a Better Human Future'. In Anthony J. Parel (ed.), *Gandhiji, Freedom and Self Rule* (pp. 139-152). New Delhi: Vistar Publications.

Howard, Ross (2006). 'The Media's Role in War and Peace Building'. In Gerd Junne and Willemijn Verkoren (eds.) *Post-conflict Development: Meeting the New Challenges (pp. 117-128).* New Delhi: Viva Books.

Jacquette, D. (2007). *Journalistic Ethics: Moral Responsibility in the Media.* Delhi: Pearson/Prentice Hall.

Jeffrey, R. (2003). *India's Newspaper Revolution: Capitalism, Politics and the Indian Language Press (Second edition),* New Delhi, Oxford University Press.

Jena, P.K. (1995). 'Effetive use of Media for Rural Development: A Study of Communication Patterns in Orissa', Ph.D. dissertation. India: Mysore University.

Karlekar, H. (2007). 'Watching the Watchdog'. In Alok Mehta

(ed.). *Indian Journalism: Keeping it Clean.* New Delhi: Rupa & Co.

Klaidman, S. and Beauchamp, T.L. (1987). *The Virtuous Journalist.* New York: Oxford University Press.

Kothari, R. (1993). *Growing Amnesia,* NewDelhi: Viking.

Krishna Murthy, N. (1966). *Indian Journalism.* Mysore: Mysore University Press.

Lee, Seow Ting and Maslog, Crispin C., (2005).' War or Peace Journalism? Asian Newspaper Coverage of conflicts', *Journal of Communication,* June, 311-329.

Mankekar, D.R. (1978). *One-way Free Flow: Neo-colonialism via News Media,* New Delhi: Clarion Books.

Mankekar, D.R. (1981). *Whose Freedom? Whose Order? A Plea for New International Information Order by Third World.* New Delhi: Clarion Books.

Masterton, M. (1998) .'A Theory of News'. In M. Breen (ed.) *Journalism: Theory and Practice* (pp. 85-103), Sydney, Macleay Press.

McGoldrick, A. and Lynch, J. (2000). *Peace Journalism: What is it? How to do it? www.reporting the world.com.*

McGoldrick, A. and Lynch, J. (2001,winter). 'What is Peace Journalism?' *Activate.*

Menefee, A. and Menefee, S. (1967) 'A Country Weekly Proves Itself in India', *Journalism Quarterly,* 44(1): 114-117.

Murthy, D.V.R. (2000). 'Development News Coverage in the Indian Press: An Analysis of Four Dailies', *Media Asia* 27(1), pp. 24-29, 53.

Murthy, D.V.R. (2001). *Developmental Journalism,* New Delhi: Dominant Publishers.

Murthy, D.V.R. (2002). *Mass Communication: Concepts and Issues,* Cochin: Olive Green Publishers.

Murthy, D.V.R. (2004). *Contemporary Press: A Study of Three Press Systems,* Visakhapatnam: Andhra University Press.

Murthy, D.V.R. (2005). *Media and Accountability,* New Delhi: Kanishka Publishers.

Murthy, D.V.R. (2006). *Development Journalism: What Next?* New Delhi: Kanishka Publishers.

Mustapha, M. (1979).'The New World Information Order'. *Journal of Communication,* 29 (2).

Nanda, B.R. (1998). *Mahatma Gandhi: A Biography* (Fifth Impression). New Delhi: Oxford University Press.

Nandy Pritish (1994a). 'Will Print Media Survive?', *Deccan Chronicle,* April 16.

Nandy Pritish (1994b). 'Goodbye Editors, Hello Marketeers', *Deccan Chronicle,* March 12.

Nayar, Kuldip (1994). 'Niminy- Piminy Press: The fourth Estate has Deviated from Principles', *Indian Express.* New Delhi, July 11.

Nelkin, D. (1987). 'The Culture of Science Journalism'. *Society,* September/October Ninan, S. (2003). 'Changing Journalism', *The Hindu,* March 2.

Ogan, C.L. (1982). 'Development Journalism/Communication: The Status of the Concept', *Gazette,* 29(1): 3-13.

Parel, Anthony J. (2002). 'Gandhian Freedoms and Self Rule'. In Anthony J. Parel (ed.),*Gandhiji, Freedom and Self Rule* (pp. 1-24). New Delhi: Vistar Publications.

Parthasarathy, R. (1991). *Modern History of Journalism in India.* New Delhi: Sterling Publishers.

Rai, U. (1992). 'Interview', in Rama Jha (ed.), *Women and Print Media: Portrayal and Performance.* New Delhi: Chanakya Publications.

Ramakrishna, C. (2002). *Historical Perspective of Press Freedom in India.* Visakhapatnam, Andhra University Press.

Ray, G.N. (2007). 'Objectivity and Accountability. In Alok Mehta (ed.). *Indian Journalism: Keeping it Clean*. New Delhi: Rupa & Co.

Rich, A.L. and Ogawa (1998). 'Intercultural and Interracial Communication: An Analytic Approach'. In G.R. Weaver (ed.). *Culture, Communication and Conflict* (pp. 54-59). Massachusetts: Simon & Schuster publishing.

Ryan, M. (2001). 'Journalistic Ethics, Objectivity, Existential Journalism, Standpoint Epistemology, and Public Journalism'. *Journal of Mass Media Ethics*, 16(1), 3-22.

Sainath, P. (1996). *Everybody Loves a Good Drought*. New Delhi: Penguin.

Sawant, P.B. (2001). 'Freedom of the Press and Ethics'. *Press Council of India Quarterly*, 22(2).

Sawant, P.B. (2003). 'Accountability in Journalism', *Journal of Mass Media Ethics*, 18(1), 16-28.

Second Press Commission of India Report (1982). New Delhi: Government of India Publication.

Selected Works of Mahatma Gandhiji Vol. 1-VI (1994) (Second popular reprint). Ahmedabad, Navajivan Trust.

Sham Lal (2003). *Indian Realities in Bits and Pieces*. New Delhi: Rupa & Co.

Shourie, A. (1995). 'Facts are Sacred, Did you Say?', *Deccan Chronicle*, June 25.

Singh, Tavleen (1994). *Hacking Away Competition'*, Indian Express, New Delhi, October 22.

Sonnenberg, U. (2004). *Regulation and Self-Regulation of the Media*, Maastricht: European Journalism Centre.

Squires, J.D. (1990). *Read all About it: The Corporate Take Over of America's Newspapers*, New York: Times Books.

Tylor, E.B. (1977). *Primitive Culture*. NewYork: Henry Holt.

Varadharajan, S. (1999). 'The Ink Link: The Media, Communalism, and the Evasion of Politics'. In K.N. Panikkar (ed.), *The Concerned India's Guide to Communalism (pp. 160-229)*. New Delhi: Penguin Books.

Vilanilam, J.V. (1975). 'Ownership vs Development News Coverage: An Analysis of Independent and Conglomerate Newspapers of India', Paper presented at AEJ convention, Ottawa.

Vilanilam, J.V. (2005). *Mass Communication in India: A Sociological Perspective*. New Delhi: Sage Publications.

Yadava, J.S. (1985). 'The Changing Social Role of Indian Press', *Media Asia, 12(3):* 111-119.

Yadava, J.S. (1991). 'Press System in India', *Media Asia, 18(3):* 132-136,142.

Wallis, T. and Samayoa, C. (2007). 'Civilian Peacekeepers: Creating a Safe Environment for Peace Building'. In Paul van Tongeren, Malin Brenk, Marte Hellena, and Juliette Verhoeven (eds.). *People Building Peace II (pp. 363-368)*. New Delhi: Viva Books.

Index